The Utopia of a Strange Love

When the Love of God Is Mishandled

Tavares D. Robinson

Published by Watchman Publishing
watchmanpublishingllc@gmail.com
1-800-714-3194

Watchman Publishing is a Christian publisher that seeks to edify the local church, by equipping individuals. We strive to provide resources that seek to admonish, exhort, reprove, and encourage the church in the Last Days.

THE UTOPIA OF A STRANGE LOVE
When the Love of God Is Mishandled

Copyright © 2018, 2020 by Tavares D. Robinson
All rights reserved.

No part of this publication may be reproduced, stored in a retrieval system, or transmitted in any form or by any means electronic, mechanical, photocopying, recording, or otherwise, without the prior written permission of the author.

Unless otherwise indicated, all Scripture references are taken from the Holy Bible, New International Version (NIV). Copyright © 1973, 1978, 1984 by International Bible Society. Used by permission of International Bible Society. All rights reserved.

Scripture quotations marked NLT are taken from the *Holy Bible*, New Living Translation, copyright © 1996, 2004, 2015 by Tyndale House Foundation. Used by permission of Tyndale House Publishers, Inc., Carol Stream, Illinois 60188. All rights reserved.

Scripture marked NKJV taken from the New King James Version®. Copyright © 1982 by Thomas Nelson. Used by permission. All rights reserved.

ISBN: 978-1-7325134-8-8

Printed in the United States of America
U.S. Printing History
First Edition: 2018
Second Edition: 2020

Dedication

This book is dedicated to the loving memory of Helen Juliette Kingcannon. Her footprints of mercy have forever changed my life. Her profound love for reading the Word of God and her steadfast devotion to prayer shall never be forgotten.

Acknowledgments

I would like to thank Leonard and Carolyn Goss for their professionalism and encouragement throughout this entire project. Len, thank you for using your skilled gifting to honor our Lord. You are truly a Baruch for our generation.

To Bart Dahmer: thank you for your guidance and your friendship. Your timely emails of prayer and support was heaven sent.

To all my family and friends whose prayers and trust means so much. Most important, my sincere indebtedness to my Lord. Thank You for allowing me to be a steward of Your message. No words can articulate how much serving You means to me. It's an honor and truly humbling to be called Your doulos.

Table of Contents

Dedication 3
Acknowledgments 4
Foreword 7
Prologue 11
The Imitation 17
Doctrine of Devils 25
When History Repeats Itself 39
The Secret Meeting 55
The Love of God 67
The Agape Deception 75
The Wrath of God 87
The Sermon on the Mount 99
The Apostle Paul 117
Is Love the Greatest? 129
The Golden Calf of Relevance 145
A Lack of Discernment 163
A Relevant Church? 175
The Mercy of God 179
Other Titles by Watchman Publishing 195

Foreword

Anyone who is conversant with scripture knows prophets get a bad rap. Indeed, they get far more than that. They are rejected, insulted, abused, hated, and even killed. The Old Testament consistently reminds us the only popular prophets are the false prophets. The masses love it when they are told what they want to hear, but they hate it when they are told what they need to hear.

Real prophets are hard to come by. As Leonard Ravenhill once put it, "The school of the prophets is never crowded."[1] Yet real prophets are needed now more than ever. Both our church and our nation are in desperate need of a strong word from God, and very few are willing to offer it. The price is high to convey biblical truth boldly, directly, and persistently. A. W. Tozer said, "The essence of the message of the prophet is truth. Truth is always a double-edged sword. It cuts both ways. There is a cost factor for the prophet to deliver the message, and there is a cost factor for us to receive that message. This emphasizes the extreme importance God puts upon the truth he is trying to bring our way."[2]

In *The Utopia of a Strange Love*, Tavares D. Robinson offers us biblical truth in the tradition of the prophets. He is well aware of the sad state of contemporary Western culture, but he puts the bulk of the blame firmly where it belongs—on the contemporary Western church. In good measure the world is in a mess today because the church is in a mess today. To work toward any sort of turnaround, we must begin with the church herself.

Such an approach is fully biblical, for, as the apostle Peter reminds us, "it is time for judgment to begin with God's household" (1 Pet. 4:17). That is what Robinson does, taking the current church to task for failing in its calling, shirking its responsibilities, caving in to the surrounding culture, falling for lousy theology, and diluting the Word of God.

It was A. W. Tozer, a towering prophetic figure Robinson often quotes, who rightly reminds us that "What comes into our minds when we think about God is the most important thing about us. The history of

---

1. Leonard Ravenhill, *Why Revival Tarries: A Classic on Revival* (Bloomington, MN: Bethany House, 2004).
2. A. W. Tozer and James L. Snyder, *Voice Of A Prophet: Who Speaks For God?* (Bloomington, MN: Bethany House, 2014).

THE UTOPIA OF A STRANGE LOVE

mankind will probably show that no people has ever risen above its religion, and man's spiritual history will positively demonstrate that no religion has ever been greater than its idea of God. Worship is pure or base as the worshiper entertains high or low thoughts of God."[3]

With this, Tavares Robinson fully concurs. Thus much of this book centers on the God with whom we have so often lost, misrepresented, or eviscerated in so much of today's Christianity. And one of the most common ways of distorting the biblical God is how we use, abuse, and misuse our understanding of the love of God. That is why this book is subtitled, "When the Love of God is Mishandled."

A great and vital doctrine like the love of God has been seriously tarnished if not trashed by many contemporary Christians. We have a thoroughly sentimental and syrupy view of the love of God, and we have isolated it from all the other divine attributes, such as His holiness, righteousness, truthfulness, and purity. Thus we have a God who is little different than sinful man and a God who basically just exists to meet our needs and keep us happy.

Robinson not only speaks much to the right (biblical) and wrong (unbiblical) understandings of God's love, but he also addresses related themes, such as the wrath of God, the holiness of God, and the like. He also spends time demolishing the false gods of our day and the crippling shibboleths we have run with, such as *tolerance*, *relevance*, and other formerly good terms now gone bad.

The author makes much of the Laodicean church, which American Christendom has sadly replicated in so many ways. As always, the only way out of this dire condition is repentance. His book concludes on this much-needed note, which if heartily entered into can bring about long-awaited revival, renewal, and reformation.

This helpful book does not just look at false teaching, bad theology, and errant views on God, Christ, and the gospel, but offers scripturally based, theologically sound, and pastorally applicable chapters on what the gospel message in fact really is. The core components of the biblical gospel are carefully laid out in *The Utopia of a Strange Love* and presented in an easy to follow fashion.

Supported by plenty of scripture references, as well as terrific quotes from some of the great men of God, this book makes its case clearly,

---

3. A. W. Tozer, *The Knowledge of the Holy* (San Francisco: HarperOne, 1978).

FOREWORD

forcefully, and unapologetically. As such, it deserves a wide hearing. But because this book dares to proclaim biblical truth in the face of growing apostasy, carnality, compromise, and worldliness, we should not expect it to be appreciated by all readers. But since when did approval of the masses, a watered-down gospel, and a craven man-pleasing message have anything to do with Christ and the kingdom?

—**Bill Muehlenberg**
CultureWatch, Melbourne, Australia

Prologue

It is not difficult discovering the dominating theme of current Christendom. The incomplete counsel of God is everywhere apparent; much of what we hear begs the question, *Where is that in the Bible?* The apostle Paul's warning concerning the Last Days is clearly playing out before us:

> In the presence of God and of Christ Jesus, who will judge the living and the dead, and in view of his appearing and his kingdom, I give you this charge: Preach the word; be prepared in season and out of season; correct, rebuke and encourage—with great patience and careful instruction. For the time will come when people will not put up with sound doctrine. Instead, to suit their own desires, they will gather around them a great number of teachers to say what their itching ears want to hear. They will turn their ears away from the truth and turn aside to myths. (2 Tim. 4:1-4)

Paul spoke a prophetic word of the time when people would no longer put up with sound doctrine and would no longer be led by the Spirit of God. Instead, they will dictate what they want to hear according to their own desires. Since their spiritual appetites will not tolerate strong meat, they will favor emotional, cotton candy teachings.

The message of this book is that those days are now here. Skilled teachers, both men and women, are available and anxious to teach the church what is desirable for the popular palate. Satan has prepared and trained his ministers cleverly to subvert the gospel with strange and damnable doctrines, all designed to tickle itching ears. What is the most frequently taught doctrine in the church today? It is the love of God according to the dictates of the world.

When the Beatles sang, "All You Need Is Love," that slogan became the church's "fight song." Love of course is an indispensable aspect of the gospel. The apostle John wrote, "Whoever does not love does not know God, because God is love" (1 John 4:8). This is true and beyond dispute. Yet it is essential that love be defined by biblical standards, not by the prevailing culture. The influence of the controlling world perspective has led the church

THE UTOPIA OF A STRANGE LOVE

to embrace an unbiblical version of love called *tolerance*. Tolerance is the allowance of beliefs or practices differing from one's own. In many cases, tolerance is an admirable thing. We should have the capacity to recognize and respect the thoughts and practices of others. Yet an overindulgence of toleration allowing for deviation from a standard leads to the dropping of all standards. When Christians drop their biblical standards to be accepted, liked, and respected by the dominate culture, this is conformity, not love.

Under the guise of toleration, we have allowed unregenerate and unsound ideas to give the church an extreme makeover. We have worked hard to appear accepting, uncritical, loving, and nonjudgmental of whatever anyone does or says. To accomplish this we replaced one error for a greater error: propagating love according to the world but ignoring the biblical definition of love. Part of Satan's end time plan is to confuse the church into substituting the secular definition of love for the concept of love taught in the Word of God. In the hands of a generation that loves self, the word *love* has become a destructive term. The word might be the same, but having the wrong definition of it can lead to worship of a different God.

Exchanging the biblical definition for the secular notion of words and concepts is the modus operandi of the enemy. Moving something that is true out of its original context in the Bible and perpetrating a new definition on the church is a dangerous trap. Nineteenth-century British pastor John Charles Ryle said that "Since Satan cannot destroy the gospel, he has too often neutralized its usefulness by addition, subtraction, or substitution."[4] One does not catch a mouse with fake cheese. Instead, real cheese is placed in a trap, thereby changing the original function of the cheese, to entice the mouse in order for the trap to kill it. In his second Epistle, the apostle Peter tells us that only diligent Christians will be the joyful Christians in the Day of the Lord. Peter warns us to be diligent in looking for the proper character of things:

> So then, dear friends, since you are looking forward to this, make every effort to be found spotless, blameless and at peace with him. Bear in mind that our Lord's patience means salvation, just as our dear brother Paul also wrote you with the wisdom that God gave him. He writes the same way in all his letters, speaking in them of these matters. His letters

---

4. J. C. Ryle, *Warnings to the Churches* (Edinburgh: Banner of Truth, 1967).

PROLOGUE

> contain some things that are hard to understand, which ignorant and unstable people distort, as they do the other Scriptures, to their own destruction. Therefore, dear friends, since you have been forewarned, be on your guard so that you may not be carried away by the error of the lawless and fall from your secure position. (2 Pet. 3:14-17)

Christians looking for the Second Coming of Christ must be on their guard to be found without spot and blameless in Christ when He comes. Being "at peace" or "in peace" means earnest diligence in rejecting discord brought by the false teachers.

Three character traits make up Satan's false teachers. First, Peter says they are ignorant. This has nothing to do with IQ or one's level of higher education. Rather, it refers to an untrained and undisciplined mind, a mind unrestrained in the interpretation of scripture. These untruthful teachers are lawless; they themselves are led away by error, and then they prey on others. Satan's teachers have little desire for the labor-intensive work of scripture exposition. They disregard the importance of context in accurate biblical interpretation. To avoid being led away by lawless teaching, we must know Christ more clearly, be more like him, and love him better. We must grow in grace, faith, virtue, and knowledge.

Second, Satan's false teachers are unstable. Being unstable means not being firm, fixed, or established. It means wavering in purpose or intent, indicating those who vacillate in their thoughts, belief, and character. An unstable teacher is one who moves along with the current trends in order to accommodate the world's perspectives or their own inner desires, proving their lack of submission to the lordship of Christ.

Third, Satan's false teachers twist or distort the teaching of scripture in favor of accepting the thoughts and opinions of men who either do not know or do not care about what God says. In the 2 Peter 3:14-17 passage, the words *ignorant* and *unstable* point to a collection of individuals demonstrating both of these characteristics simultaneously. The result of such scripture twisting is destruction, for deceptive teachers put themselves and others in great danger of rejecting the truth. The word *distort* means to twist, to torment, and to overstretch. It comes from an instrument—a winch—that was used to produce torture by twisting or pulling a person's limbs out of joint. In the passage from 2 Peter, the Holy Spirit chose to use

THE UTOPIA OF A STRANGE LOVE

a graphic and violent term to illustrate the perverted and diabolical nature of scripture twisting.

In the hands of Satan's deceitful teachers, scripture twisting is not done by mistake. It is on purpose and intentional. Peter prophetically warned us that men will come and distort the Word of God. They will use scripture like the victims of torture, forcing the Bible to say what they want it to say. They will interject philosophical, obstinate opinions, denominational persuasions, and culturally biased meanings on God's Word, all in an effort to alternate its original meaning. Christian apologist Jewel van der Merwe said, "When we leave the parameters of the Word of God, we drift onto the sea of subjectivity. In this sea, spirituality becomes relative to whatever new revelation or vision that comes forth."[5]

Peter warns us that the consequence of being led away by error is eternal ruin. "[Paul's] letters contain some things that are hard to understand, which ignorant and unstable people distort, as they do the other scriptures, to their own destruction" (2 Pet. 3:16). There is the story about an art enthusiast who displayed a collection of etchings on his office walls, including one of the Leaning Tower of Pisa. Each morning he noticed it was crooked, so he straightened it. Finally one evening he asked the cleaning woman if she was responsible for moving the picture each night. "Why, yes," she said. "I have to hang it crooked to make the tower straight!" This is what is happening to the church. Cultural relevance has caused many people to think rearranging and modifying the Bible can redefine love to make it more presentable and more acceptable to a self-centered generation.

A fatally destructive disease called apostasy is spreading throughout the body of Christ. It is producing signs of a strange love, a love produced from human imagination that is not on familiar terms with the Bible. If God embraced today's view of love, one would wonder why Satan got kicked out of heaven in the first place. Or why the prophet Isaiah wrote that "it was the Lord's will to crush him [Christ] and cause him to suffer" (Isa. 53:10). If scripture supported the secular version of love, it would beg the question, *Was Isaiah a prophet at all?*

Paul told us that it is only when we speak the truth plainly that we minister on God's behalf. He wrote, "Therefore, since through God's mercy we have this ministry, we do not lose heart. Rather, we have renounced secret and shameful ways; we do not use deception, nor do we distort the word of

---

5. Jewel van der Merwe, "The Sea of Subjectivity," March/April 1999.

PROLOGUE

God. On the contrary, by setting forth the truth plainly we commend ourselves to everyone's conscience in the sight of God" (2 Cor. 4:1-2). God has given us a job to do, and it is not through our own doing but through his loving-kindness. So we do not give up. We put away things done in secret and shame. We do not play with the Word of God or use it in a false way. Because we tell the truth, and only because we tell the truth, men and women who are sincere will want to listen to us.

Paul's appeal to set forth the truth plainly is the inspiration for *The Utopia of a Strange Love: When the Love of God is Mishandled*. While countless numbers are drinking in a new and subversive version of the love of God, the authentic love of God compels me to sit in silence no longer. To remain speechless while souls are eternally destroyed is to succumb to evil. American pastor and Bible scholar Walter J. Chantry once said, "When truth is silent, false views seem plausible."[6] I have written this book to arouse those willing to listen. The words of British novelist and scriptwriter Dresden James ring loud in my soul: "A truth's initial commotion is directly proportional to how deeply the lie was believed. It wasn't the world being round that agitated people, but that the world wasn't flat. When a well-packaged web of lies has been sold gradually to masses over generations, the truth will seem utterly preposterous and its speaker a raving lunatic."[7]

Zeal, mixed with the true knowledge of God, is urgently needed in our day. The enemy has groomed many latter-day landmark removers within the body of Christ; therefore I feel duty-bound to proclaim God's truth regardless of the criticism or insults. Just as the Word of God was rare in days past (1 Sam. 3:1 tells us, "In those days the word of the Lord was rare; there were not many visions"), so historical truth is rare today. Yet I sense the Spirit of God speaking to the church and revealing it is time to turn around and rediscover the ancient ways. I pray this book stirs repentance in the hearts of those who have embraced a false love. I pray it strengthens and encourages the hearts of those who have suffered much affliction for their biblical stand concerning God's love. I pray it ignites a godly jealousy for the bride of Christ to be presented without spot or blemish.

---

6. Walter J. Chantry, *Today's Gospel: Authentic or Synthetic* (Edinburgh: Banner of Truth, 1970).
7. Source unknown.

THE IMITATION

Before what students of the Bible refer to as "the fall of man," when the first man and the first woman, who were in a state of innocence, disobeyed the command of God, there was an earlier fall that took place in heaven. I refer to the fall of Satan, which occurred somewhere after God created the angels and before Satan tempted Adam and Eve in the Garden of Eden. God cast Satan out of heaven, along with a third of the angels who followed him. Isaiah 14:15 says, "But you [Satan] are brought down to the realm of the dead, to the depths of the pit." Because of pride, which was the sin of Satan's fallen nature, Satan was pushed, or thrown, from heaven. Ezekiel 28:16-17 records how this happened: "Through your widespread trade you were filled with violence, and you sinned. So I drove you in disgrace from the mount of God, and I expelled you, guardian cherub, from among the fiery stones. Your heart became proud on account of your beauty, and you corrupted your wisdom because of your splendor. So I threw you to the earth; I made a spectacle of you before kings." Spiritual pride of the devil and those filled with this same spiritual pride can expect to perish.

Though Isaiah 14 addresses the king of Babylon, it is also referring to Satan, our chief adversary. In verses 12-14, we have a glimpse into the heart of Satan and what caused his removal from heaven:

> How you have fallen from heaven, morning star, son of the dawn! You have been cast down to the earth, you who once laid low the nations! You said in your heart, "I will ascend to the heavens; I will raise my throne above the stars of God; I will sit enthroned on the mount of assembly, on the utmost heights of Mount Zaphon. I will ascend above the tops of the clouds; I will make myself like the Most High." (Isa. 14:12-14)

"I will ascend to the heavens." "I will raise my throne." "I will sit enthroned . . . on the utmost heights." "I will ascend above the tops." "I will make myself like the Most High." These verses reveal the stark love and sheer pride of self that led to Satan's downfall. The love of self and pride are in

THE UTOPIA OF A STRANGE LOVE

fact the two evils always associated with someone deserting the faith. What was Satan's goal and desire? "I will ascend above the tops of the clouds; I will make myself like the Most High." His objective was to be like God, equal in power, worship, authority, and reverence. When Lucifer was removed from heaven, God then created humans to live for and glorify Him. Now Satan's target became God's new creation.

The adversary appears as a crafty serpent in the Garden of Eden, craftier than any of the wild animals the Lord God had made (Gen. 3:1). In other places in scripture, we see him depicted as various creatures, including a dragon. The twelfth chapter of Revelation has an end-time description of the dragon and the serpent. "Then war broke out in heaven. Michael and his angels fought against the dragon, and the dragon and his angels fought back. But he was not strong enough, and they lost their place in heaven. The great dragon was hurled down—that ancient serpent called the devil, or Satan, who leads the whole world astray. He was hurled to the earth, and his angels with him" (Rev. 12:7-9). As the dragon, Satan is the one who persecutes the sons and daughters of God with ferocity and cruelty. He is "the accuser of our brothers and sisters, who accuses them before our God day and night" (Rev. 12:10). As the serpent, he is the great deceiver, "that ancient serpent called the devil, or Satan, who leads the whole world astray" (Rev. 12:9).

If affliction and opposition do not work in making Christians bow to Satan, his next move is craftiness. In the third chapter of Genesis, the serpent, who is called the most crafty creature the Lord made, deceived Eve in order to lead her and her husband into sin. Ultimately, that deception caused the original pair to disobey what God said: "When the woman saw that the fruit of the tree was good for food and pleasing to the eye, and also desirable for gaining wisdom, she took some and ate it. She also gave some to her husband, who was with her, and he ate it" (Gen. 3:6). It was then that the eyes of both Adam and Eve opened to what they had done. Because our human parents failed to obey God's original commandment, sin entered into the human race.

Before God removed Adam and Eve from the garden, He cursed Satan and prophesied that there would be constant enmity between Satan's seed and Christ's seed. "So the Lord God said to the serpent, 'Because you have done this, "Cursed are you above all livestock and all wild animals! . . . I will put enmity between you and the woman, and between your offspring and hers; he will crush your head, and you will strike his heel"'" (Gen. 3:14-15).

From that point on, people of every generation have struggled with the Fall. "We know that we are children of God, and that the whole world is under the control of the evil one," according to the apostle John (1 John 5:19).

The good news in all this is that enmity with the enemy of God opens up the possibility of restoring friendship with God, made possible by the seed or offspring of the woman—the coming of the Messiah, the promised Deliverer that the rest of the Bible reveals. In the end, "The great dragon was hurled down—that ancient serpent called the devil, or Satan, who leads the whole world astray. He was hurled to the earth, and his angels with him" (Rev. 12:9).

Satan's great desire has always been to imitate God and to receive worship like God, and his way of receiving that worship has been to deceive. Revivalist and author Vance Havner once said, "He [Satan] accomplishes more by imitation than by outright opposition."[8] The root of spiritual deception is when we perceive something to be acceptable by God's standards but, really, they measure up to our own standards instead. Satan's ploy in this is to convince us we are worshiping God when we are actually worshiping our own desires and exalting them above God's plans. The adversary seeks to subvert the Word of God and convince believers they can have their own way. He gives a false sense of serving God, knowing God would never deviate from His established and revealed will. This is how deception works. It never appears as deception; it has to appear real, as truth—just enough truth to be believable but studded with error to make it deadly. It is a total imitation.

SATAN THE IMITATOR

I watched a football game, and it was time for the marching bands to perform. As one of the bands took the field, someone announced, "We are always imitated but never duplicated." Satan's modus operandi is to imitate every move of God. Let us not forget that his ambition is to be worshipped as God. Scholar and author C. S. Lewis once said, "There is no

---

8. Dennis J. Hester, *The Vance Havner Quote Book* (Grand Rapids: Baker Publishing Group, 1986).

THE UTOPIA OF A STRANGE LOVE

neutral ground in the universe. Every square inch, every split second is claimed by God and counter claimed by Satan."[9]

There is no end to the ways Satan imitates God, even to the forming of an unholy trinity of the antichrist, the beast, and the false prophet in the end times. "And the devil, who deceived them, was thrown into the lake of burning sulfur, where the beast and the false prophet had been thrown. They will be tormented day and night for ever and ever" (Rev. 20:10). Christ revealed Himself as the Light of the world, and in this way also Satan imitates; Paul tells us that "Satan himself masquerades as an angel of light" (2 Cor. 11:4). When imitating the Lord like this, Satan will not appear as an angel of hate and division but rather as an angel of encouragement and unity.

Other examples of Satan's pattern of imitation include the "people of the evil one" merging with "the good seed [that] stands for the people of the kingdom" in the parable of the wheat and tares (Matt. 13:38). As the Lord raised up and sent out His apostles, Satan likewise sends out his deceitful workers: "For such people are false apostles, deceitful workers, masquerading as apostles of Christ" (2 Cor. 11:13). As Jesus is seated upon a throne, so is Satan: "I know where you live—where Satan has his throne" (Rev. 2:13). Satan imitates Christ in the performance of miracles: "For false messiahs and false prophets will appear and perform great signs and wonders to deceive, if possible, even the elect" (Matt. 24:24); "The coming of the lawless one will be in accordance with how Satan works. He will use all sorts of displays of power through signs and wonders that serve the lie" (2 Thess. 2:9). The last example contrasts Satan's "secret power of lawlessness" (2 Thess. 2:7) with "the mystery from which true godliness springs" (1 Tim. 3:16). Satan's plan is to merge his works, name, and power with God so he can be worshipped.

THE DISTORTION OF GOD'S LOVE

As we draw closer to the return of Christ, Satan will increasingly appear as angel of light to cause a great falling away. The New King James Version says, "Let no man deceive you by any means: for that day shall not come, except there come a falling away first, and that man of sin be revealed, the son of perdition" (2 Thess. 2:3). In a culture that loves self and pleasure,

---

9. C. S. Lewis, *The Lion, The Witch and The Wardrobe* (Broadway, NY: HarperCollins, 2002).

the enemy's focus during the end times will be on distorting the true nature of God's love. By twisting the meaning of love, every other foundation of faith and belief is distorted—with eternal consequences.

Many people say they believe in the concept of the love of God. However, how many believe in the doctrine of hell? Or the wrath of God? Or the lordship of Christ? Satan is well aware what teachings are popular and attract the most listeners. The more lenient the teaching, the better, for his purposes. That way, evil looks harmless. He will stick with *positivity*, and that is why he majors in the things that involve little difficulty or discomfort.

In these Last Days, truth and error will be preached in the same pulpits, attend the same churches, live in the same houses, and travel on the same pathway. The job of our adversary will be to help the multitudes confuse evil with good—to make sure error looks and sounds just like the truth. Through the prophet Isaiah, the Bible says, "Woe to those who call evil good and good evil, who put darkness for light and light for darkness, who put bitter for sweet and sweet for bitter" (Isa. 5:20). The original human pair was confused, and due to the work of Satan, men and women have been confused since.

The only defense we have against the great deceiver is the Word of God, explained, expounded, exalted, and defended.

SEDUCING SPIRITS

The study of eschatology is concerned with understanding the final events of the world. The word is composed of two Greek terms, *eschatos*, meaning last, and *logos*, meaning word or to reason. Together they mean "the study of the Last Days" or "the final things of the church and kingdom age." Over the years, the subject of eschatology has taken a spiritual thrashing. In some circles, it is despised because untruthful teachers, many of them televangelists, have promoted biased and unscriptural ideas that numb and blind people to the reality of Christ's coming. Personally, I believe this was all part of Satan's plan.

In speaking about His coming, Jesus gives us two unique pictures of desensitized spiritual discernment in the Last Days when He compares the days of Noah and the days of Lot to the days of the Son of Man:

> Just as it was in the days of Noah, so also will it be in the days of the Son of Man. People were eating, drinking,

> marrying and being given in marriage up to the day Noah entered the ark. Then the flood came and destroyed them all. It was the same in the days of Lot. People were eating and drinking, buying and selling, planting and building. But the day Lot left Sodom, fire and sulfur rained down from heaven and destroyed them all. It will be just like this on the day the Son of Man is revealed. (Luke 17:26-30)

Why was judgment exacted on the cultures of Noah and Lot? Jesus does not mention the gross sins of those cultures because He was talking to people who knew why there was judgment. Instead, He focuses on the apathy and self-centered lives of those living in those days. Scripture says they ate, drank, bought, married, sold, planted, and built. They were times of overwhelming spiritual delusion—"business as usual." The Lord tells us, "It will be just like this on the day the Son of Man is revealed." In the pursuit of happiness, people will be living their lives to the fullest, loving who they are, and living their best lives. It is very alarming that these moments determine humankind's eternal existence, and when they burst upon the scene they will be anything but business as usual.

What the Holy Spirit Says

Scriptural eschatology is essential for the church today. It not only gives us hope in trying and difficult days but it also gives us a clear sense of what is coming. We do not need to be unprepared or caught off guard by the things that have been foretold. One of those things has to do with deceiving or seducing spirits. In 1 Timothy 4:1-2, the apostle Paul writes, "The Spirit clearly says that in later times some will abandon the faith and follow deceiving spirits and things taught by demons. Such teachings come through hypocritical liars, whose consciences have been seared as with a hot iron." These verses show us how Satan's view of love will be accepted as God's love—seducing spirits influencing false prophets. These fraudulent prophets will tell lies with straight faces and do it so often their consciences will not even bother them. They, and those who follow them, will depart from the faith as unfeeling flesh seared by hot irons.

When Paul indicates, "the Spirit clearly says," he is not making this up. He has become an oracle through which the Spirit communicates to the church. The apostle Peter speaks to this subject as well: "Above all, you must understand that no prophecy of Scripture came about by the prophet's own interpretation of things. For prophecy never had its origin in the human will, but prophets, though human, spoke from God as they were carried along by the Holy Spirit" (2 Pet. 1:20-21). What the Spirit says to Paul is said clearly, openly, directly, and explicitly in well-defined words. There should be no misunderstanding on what the Spirit is communicating. He is repeating now what has been spoken before.

When we learn that "in later times some will abandon the faith," Paul is speaking about a period following his current time of writing. During this time, people will ignore the church, defect from the truth, and take the wrong path. There may be a profession of Christianity, but they will deny essential doctrinal truths. In other words, they will apostatize—deliberately decide to abandon truths they once counted dear for something contrary to the truth. What do they abandon? The faith. Paul is not referring here to Christian professions. He is talking about Christian doctrine, the body of teachings that has not changed throughout history. It is the same faith Jude mentions in his Epistle: "Dear friends, although I was very eager to write to you about the salvation we share, I felt compelled to write and urge you to contend for the faith that was once for all entrusted to God's holy people" (Jude 3).

The idea of deceiving or seducing spirits comes the Greek word *planos*, from which we get our word *planet*. It means to wander or to rove. There are evil, supernatural spirits whose objective is to lead people astray by causing them to wander from the truth. These spirits constantly lead in a way that has no fixed destination. They are misleading and deceiving spirits.

When 1 Timothy 4:1 mentions "things taught by demons," the reference is not to the doctrine of demons or to demonology, which is teaching *on* demons. What it relates to is teachings inspired, suggested, and done *by* demons—teachings formulated by Satan, who uses other people's mouths to be the mouthpieces of error. "Such teachings come through hypocritical liars," according to Paul when writing to Timothy. This denotes those who appear authentic but are really pretenders and imposters. It is through this role that they speak false truths. These deceitful teachers are addicted to the lies they tell. They are like the Pharisees, whom Jesus called hypocrites seven times in the twenty-third chapter of Matthew's Gospel alone. They are all about deceiving and distorting the gospel of Christ and ruining the souls of men and women. They do this with consciences "seared as with a hot iron," cauterized, deadened, and without feelings.

THE UTOPIA OF A STRANGE LOVE

This Is Happening Now

God has chosen the church to spread the truth in the world. What is truth? It is the revelation of Jesus Christ, which is the mystery of godliness. Scriptural eschatology teaches that in a certain period before the return of Jesus Christ, people in the church will abandon the essential teachings of the faith and follow deceiving spirits. They will walk away from the doctrinal truths they once believed wholeheartedly and accept the spurious anti-gospel of Satan and his lying prophets. Characteristically, false teachers have a verbal confession of faith—a show and form of godliness—but this is a masquerade. Inwardly they disdain the weightier matters of the gospel; they have no taste for doctrine. Their form of godliness is a cloak for wickedness, for they are ministers of Satan.

Satan empowers his lieutenants, gives them a platform to articulate their teachings, and aids them in their task of redefining and supplanting the original, historical views of the church. The more successful false teachers will be men and women of popularity and charisma, all the better to spread the devil's damnable teachings. Because they are so addicted to the lies they spread, they do it without any conviction or remorse.

Look around, people of God. This is happening among us right now. The scriptures we have just examined in this brief chapter are the foundational scriptures for the rest of this book. We must understand what the Spirit is saying to the church. If we fail in this regard, we will find ourselves roving aimlessly like spiritual vagabonds, drifting toward every new thing tickling our itching ears. But that way leads to destruction.

> But there were also false prophets among the people, just as there will be false teachers among you. They will secretly introduce destructive heresies, even denying the sovereign Lord who bought them—bringing swift destruction on themselves. Many will follow their depraved conduct and will bring the way of truth into disrepute. In their greed these teachers will exploit you with fabricated stories. Their condemnation has long been hanging over them, and their destruction has not been sleeping. (2 Pet. 2: 1-3)

DOCTRINE OF DEVILS

> Bad theology dishonors God and hurts people. Churches that sever the root of truth may flourish for a season, but they will wither eventually or turn into something besides a Christian church.[10]

Pastor and theologian John Piper makes a powerful and important statement about bad theology. Theology is for all of us, not just those who study in theological seminaries and divinity schools. All who follow Christ should study theology. Christian theology is the understanding of who God is as He reveals Himself in the scriptures. It is accomplished by immersing oneself in the Word of God to discover what God has revealed about Himself. Like so many other biblical terms, however, theology has been mocked, degraded, and thought of as something outmoded and merely intellectual.

Bad theology is essentially bad doctrine. Because it paints a wrong picture of whom God is and what pleases and displeases Him, it most certainly dishonors God and hurts people. Danger is always lurking behind erroneous teachings. The bad teaching now making the rounds is not necessarily coming from men and women who are ignorant or just misinformed. They know very well what they are doing. They are disseminating disinformation not misinformation. Misinformation is an accidental untruth, usually corrected when the truth is learned. Disinformation, on the other hand, is intentional, hiding another agenda to misrepresent the truth. When those who spread disinformation hear the truth, they reject it and withdraw from those who question them.

The "things taught by demons" that Paul mentions in 1 Timothy 4:1 are not referencing human mistakes. Paul is speaking of people under the direct influence of deceiving spirits who intentionally teach to mislead and present counterfeit truths. Deceiving through perverted or twisted truths has been Satan's foray all the way from "Has God indeed said . . . ?" to quoting

---

10. John Piper, "Destruction Is not Sleeping," May 23, 1982, message from the Desiring God website.

scripture to Christ in the wilderness: "It is written . . ." As we find in Jude 4, "Certain individuals whose condemnation was written about long ago have secretly slipped in among you. They are ungodly people, who pervert the grace of our God into a license for immorality and deny Jesus Christ our only Sovereign and Lord."

Seducing and lying spirits will greatly intensify leading up to the return of Christ. In Jewish teachings there is a phrase called *Kal va-homer*, meaning light and heavy. *Kal va-homer* is also an exegetical principle assuming that what applies in a lenient case inescapably applies in a stricter case. For our purposes, deception has always been around (light), so how much more will it be intensified in the end times (heavy)? These seducing spirits and the doctrines they preach will be the driving force in end time apostasy. The Bible does not promise a great harvest of souls coming into the church, but it does declare a great falling away.

The Olivet Discourse

Jesus' teaching in Matthew 24, called the Olivet Discourse, speaks with clarity on the signs of His coming at the end of the age. The Lord tells His disciples about the coming destruction of the great and impressive temple, which was ten stories high and decorated with gold and silver. Jesus prophesied it would be reduced to rubble. He said, "Not one stone here will be left on another; every one will be thrown down" (Matt. 24:2). His words shocked the disciples because they believed the temple had to stand for all Jewish prophecies to be fulfilled. What they heard was contrary to their belief system. Yet forty years later, the Roman soldiers surrounded Jerusalem and leveled the city and the temple.

The disciples asked, "Tell us . . . when will this happen, and what will be the sign of your coming and of the end of the age?" Jesus answered,

> Watch out that no one deceives you. For many will come in my name, claiming, "I am the Messiah," and will deceive many. You will hear of wars and rumors of wars, but see to it that you are not alarmed. Such things must happen, but the end is still to come. Nation will rise against nation, and kingdom against kingdom. There will be famines and earthquakes in various places. All these are the beginning of birth pains. Then you will be handed over to be persecuted

THE DOCTRINE OF DEVILS

and put to death, and you will be hated by all nations because of me. At that time many will turn away from the faith and will betray and hate each other, and many false prophets will appear and deceive many people. Because of the increase of wickedness, the love of most will grow cold, but the one who stands firm to the end will be saved. And this gospel of the kingdom will be preached in the whole world as a testimony to all nations, and then the end will come. So when you see standing in the holy place "the abomination that causes desolation," spoken of through the prophet Daniel—let the reader understand—then let those who are in Judea flee to the mountains. Let no one on the housetop go down to take anything out of the house. Let no one in the field go back to get their cloak. How dreadful it will be in those days for pregnant women and nursing mothers! Pray that your flight will not take place in winter or on the Sabbath. For then there will be great distress, unequaled from the beginning of the world until now—and never to be equaled again. If those days had not been cut short, no one would survive, but for the sake of the elect those days will be shortened. At that time if anyone says to you, "Look, here is the Messiah!" or, "There he is!" do not believe it. For false messiahs and false prophets will appear and perform great signs and wonders to deceive, if possible, even the elect. (Matt. 24:4-24)

The word *deceive* is used four times in this text. In fact, when talking about the signs of His coming, Jesus spoke about end time deception four times more than any other subject. Almost every New Testament book warns us in some way about deception, but this book in particular raises the level of seriousness very high. Deception perpetrated on the church is a dire thing. Yet when someone sounds the alarm in the church today, often they are called "critical" or "heresy hunters." The warning about end time deception, however, is more relevant today than it was in the first century. Think of obvious cults like the Jehovah's Witnesses or the Mormons. Think of the man on the street claiming he is Jesus. When Jesus said, "Many will come in my name, claiming, 'I am the Messiah,' and will deceive many," he was not necessarily speaking about the man who says he is Christ. The key idea here is, "Many will come in my name." Jesus said people will come *in*

27

THE UTOPIA OF A STRANGE LOVE

His name, not *with* His name. They will not come to assume His identity but to presume to represent Him. To go in someone's name means going in their place, standing as their representative and authorized to speak on behalf of them. Jesus is warning us about men and women who claim they are sent by Christ to speak on His behalf.

"Watch out that no one deceives you. For many will come in my name," warns the Lord. Not a few but many will come in His name. The word used for "many" in the New Testament Greek is *polýs* or *polus*, and it means great in numbers—even a majority. The same word is used by the apostle John in Revelation 7:9, "After this I looked, and there before me was a *great multitude* that no one could count, from every nation, tribe, people and language, standing before the throne and before the Lamb."(emphasis added). The word emphasizes the great quantity of a thing. With that in mind, Jesus is warning us that in the end times, a great throng of people will come saying they represent Him and are authorized by Him to speak on His behalf. In what way shall they say this? In their teachings!

We have a similar warning from the apostle Paul, who in his second Epistle to Timothy wrote, "In fact, everyone who wants to live a godly life in Christ Jesus will be persecuted, while evildoers and impostors will go from bad to worse, deceiving and being deceived" (3:12-13). A large volume of false teachers will come with teachings supposedly from the Lord, but they are teachings that will deceive many. The Greek word to describe the deceivers is the same word to describe those who are deceived. This is why Christ is warning the disciples and us that danger is on the horizon. A biblical style of love warns the neighbor headed for danger. Jesus warned and did not flatter the disciples about the seriousness of the times, and neither should we. When Jesus taught His disciples, He taught to build them in faith. He did not want what He taught them—what He was building within them—to be lost through Satan's craftiness.

Jesus said that many false prophets would appear and deceive many people. He placed a title, an identification, on those who claim they have come in His name but who were never sent. The reason the Lord called them false prophets was because that was the term used by the Hebrew prophets when they addressed a nation in apostasy. Dating back to the days of Elijah, false prophets were to blame for times of spiritual decline and deception. They have been Satan's workers for ages, and Jesus assures us that will continue until His return. When God's people moved backward instead of forward, it was because they listened to and believed those who God had not sent.

Jeremiah Weighs In

God raised up the prophet Jeremiah specifically to confront the false prophets God's own people embraced. Jeremiah's messages give us a straightforward picture of how God views the situation:

> A horrible and shocking thing has happened in the land: The prophets prophesy lies, the priests rule by their own authority, and my people love it this way. But what will you do in the end? (Jer. 5:30-31)

> But I said, "Alas, Sovereign Lord! The prophets keep telling them, 'You will not see the sword or suffer famine. Indeed, I will give you lasting peace in this place.'" Then the Lord said to me, "The prophets are prophesying lies in my name. I have not sent them or appointed them or spoken to them. They are prophesying to you false visions, divinations, idolatries and the delusions of their own minds. (Jer. 14:13-14)

> Among the prophets of Samaria I saw this repulsive thing: They prophesied by Baal and led my people Israel astray. And among the prophets of Jerusalem I have seen something horrible: They commit adultery and live a lie. They strengthen the hands of evildoers, so that not one of them turns from their wickedness. They are all like Sodom to me; the people of Jerusalem are like Gomorrah. Therefore this is what the Lord Almighty says concerning the prophets: "I will make them eat bitter food and drink poisoned water, because from the prophets of Jerusalem ungodliness has spread throughout the land." This is what the Lord Almighty says: "Do not listen to what the prophets are prophesying to you; they fill you with false hopes. They speak visions from their own minds, not from the mouth of the Lord. They keep saying to those who despise me, 'The Lord says: You will have peace.' And to all who follow the stubbornness of their hearts they say, 'No harm will come to you.'" (Jer. 23:13-17)

THE UTOPIA OF A STRANGE LOVE

I did not send these prophets, yet they have run with their message; I did not speak to them, yet they have prophesied. (Jer. 23:21)

I have heard what the prophets say who prophesy lies in my name. They say, "I had a dream! I had a dream!" How long will this continue in the hearts of these lying prophets, who prophesy the delusions of their own minds? They think the dreams they tell one another will make my people forget my name, just as their ancestors forgot my name through Baal worship. (Jer. 23:25-27)

"Indeed, I am against those who prophesy false dreams," declares the Lord. "They tell them and lead my people astray with their reckless lies, yet I did not send or appoint them. They do not benefit these people in the least," declares the Lord. (Jer. 23:32)

Do not listen to the words of the prophets who say to you, "You will not serve the king of Babylon," for they are prophesying lies to you. "I have not sent them," declares the Lord. "They are prophesying lies in my name. Therefore, I will banish you and you will perish, both you and the prophets who prophesy to you." (Jer. 27:14-15)

Then the prophet Jeremiah said to Hananiah the prophet, "Listen, Hananiah! The Lord has not sent you, yet you have persuaded this nation to trust in lies. Therefore this is what the Lord says: 'I am about to remove you from the face of the earth. This very year you are going to die, because you have preached rebellion against the Lord.'" (Jer. 28:15-16)

Yes, this is what the Lord Almighty, the God of Israel, says: "Do not let the prophets and diviners among you deceive you. Do not listen to the dreams you encourage them to have. They are prophesying lies to you in my name. I have not sent them," declares the Lord. (Jer. 29:8-9)

THE DOCTRINE OF DEVILS

> The visions of your prophets were false and worthless; they did not expose your sin to ward off your captivity. The prophecies they gave you were false and misleading. (Lam. 2:14)

The prophet Jeremiah undertook a daunting task in confronting the false prophets. God sent him to stop people from developing an ear for false messengers. He was up against Satan, who, since the time of ancient Israel, always used false prophets to move God's people off their intended course. As the saying goes, "Satan has no new games, just different players." He selects men and women who have a good presentation, enough "truth" to be believable, and enough error to be lethal. The greatest threat to the church is internal—not external.

Just as in modern-day terrorism, so is the false prophet in the church. Catching a terrorist is hard because of their ability to blend in. They look like upright citizens, and they speak like them too. Their objective is to stay undercover until the time comes to take lives. False prophets work the same way. Jesus said, "Watch out for false prophets. They come to you in sheep's clothing, but inwardly they are ferocious wolves" (Matt. 7:15). The apostle Paul said, "And no wonder, for Satan himself masquerades as an angel of light" (2 Cor. 11:14). It is not a difficult thing for Satan's emissaries to transform themselves into what the uninitiated think of as ministers of righteousness. False prophets never appear to be false, and that is what makes them so devious and dangerous. It is their teachings and beliefs however that prove them to be false.

A prophet is someone who lends his voice on behalf of God as a spokesperson for God. A false prophet is one who tries assuming the role of a true prophet but is a phony. The New Testament word for false prophet is *pseudoprophetes*. Pseudoprophetes are those who claim to be prophets of God when they actually prophesy falsely. They utter falsehoods under the name of divine truth. In the Old Testament, this term, *false prophet,* was giving to men when their prophecy did not come to pass—or if it came to pass but turned people away from God:

> If a prophet, or one who foretells by dreams, appears among you and announces to you a sign or wonder, and if the sign or wonder spoken of takes place, and the prophet says, "Let us follow other gods" [gods you have not known] "and let us

worship them," you must not listen to the words of that prophet or dreamer. The Lord your God is testing you to find out whether you love him with all your heart and with all your soul. It is the Lord your God you must follow, and him you must revere. Keep his commands and obey him; serve him and hold fast to him. That prophet or dreamer must be put to death for inciting rebellion against the Lord your God. (Deut. 13:1-5)

Peter on False Prophets

In New Testament times, being a false prophet meant teaching wrong doctrines in the name of God. This was Jesus' definition in the twenty-fourth chapter of Matthew when he said false prophets would appear and deceive many people. He was referring to those who teach unbiblical and perverse things to turn people's hearts from God. The apostle Peter also deals with false teachers and their ultimate destruction:

> But there were also false prophets among the people, just as there will be false teachers among you. They will secretly introduce destructive heresies, even denying the sovereign Lord who bought them—bringing swift destruction on themselves. Many will follow their depraved conduct and will bring the way of truth into disrepute. In their greed these teachers will exploit you with fabricated stories. Their condemnation has long been hanging over them, and their destruction has not been sleeping. (2 Pet. 2:1-3)

The Lord Jesus ascended to heaven thirty years prior to Peter writing these verses. Times had changed, and Peter knew his days were ending. He had been an eyewitness to countless miracles as well as the teachings of Christ. The love for Christ and His church was stamped on Peter's heart. He knew what it was like to be forgiven; he never forgot the humbling encounter he had with the Savior on the shores of Galilee:

> When they had finished eating, Jesus said to Simon Peter, "Simon son of John, do you love me more than these?" "Yes, Lord," he said, "you know that I love you." Jesus said, "Feed my lambs." Again Jesus said, "Simon son of John, do you

love me?" He answered, "Yes, Lord, you know that I love you." Jesus said, "Take care of my sheep." The third time he said to him, "Simon son of John, do you love me?" Peter was hurt because Jesus asked him the third time, "Do you love me?" He said, "Lord, you know all things; you know that I love you." Jesus said, "Feed my sheep. (John 21:15-17)

As Peter approached death, the Lord's admonition to "feed my sheep" was still ringing loud and clear in his battered and tested soul. At the end of his life, the apostle left a warning that only true prophets were led by the Holy Spirit to write the scriptures:

> Above all, you must understand that no prophecy of Scripture came about by the prophet's own interpretation of things. For prophecy never had its origin in the human will, but prophets, though human, spoke from God as they were carried along by the Holy Spirit. (2 Pet. 1:20-21)

Peter made it very clear that no true prophet was ever led by his or her own will or feelings. Instead, they were moved, "carried along by the Holy Spirit," under the divine influence of God.

Peter begins the second chapter of his second letter by contrasting those who were sent by God, therefore under the Holy Spirit direction, and those who were not sent by God but went out under the influence of another spirit. There is a major conflict within the church, and Peter uses vivid and terrifying images to show the seriousness of Satan's "hit men" who will be turned loose against the body of Christ. John Piper states, "Chapter one is mainly an encouragement to avail ourselves of God's power to lead lives of godliness and love. Chapter two is mainly a warning against the destruction that will befall those who don't avail themselves of this power. If chapter one is the carrot, chapter two is the crack of the whip over our heads. There are no commands, no admonitions, no imperatives in chapter two; just pure, terrifying description of what will happen to those who fall prey to the false teachers in the church."[11]

As I have said, a false prophet—pseudoprophetes—is one who pretends to be sent by God and who pretends to speak on God's behalf. The

---

11. Ibid.

THE UTOPIA OF A STRANGE LOVE

apostle Peter is drawing his readers back to the former days when Israel was constantly engaged with false prophets. These prophets did not operate from the outside but from within. That is, they arose from within Israel itself and not from the pagans or Gentiles. Peter's message is that in the same way false teachers appeared among God's chosen people in the past, these evil people will appear among the church. We have to face them. It is not the Muslims, Jehovah's Witnesses, or any other group denying the deity of Christ and the scriptures we need to fear most. No, we have been forewarned about men and women who talk our talk, read our Bibles, speak our language, sing our songs, and proclaim our salvation.

Just as the false prophets misrepresented God in Israel, they will misrepresent God in the church. Peter uses another word for these interlopers: *pseudodidaskalos*. It is a compound word meaning a cunning or crafty teacher, one who lays out a pattern to be followed. The root word *didasko* means to teach so as to shape or bend the will of the one being taught. When we put this all together, we have a clear definition of a false teacher as a cunning and crafty teacher who appears to be an authentic and true teacher but who teaches deadly doctrines designed to shape the will of the listeners. As sure as Christ came, died, rose from the dead, and ascended to the right hand of the Father, we know that false teachers will come. The apostle Paul warned the elders at Ephesus about the coming deception they too would face:

> For I have not hesitated to proclaim to you the whole will of God. Keep watch over yourselves and all the flock of which the Holy Spirit has made you overseers. Be shepherds of the church of God, which he bought with his own blood. I know that after I leave, savage wolves will come in among you and will not spare the flock. Even from your own number men will arise and distort the truth in order to draw away disciples after them. So be on your guard! Remember that for three years I never stopped warning each of you night and day with tears. Now I commit you to God and to the word of his grace, which can build you up and give you an inheritance among all those who are sanctified (Acts 20:27-32).

W. A. Criswell defines a false teacher as "A suave, affable, personable, scholarly man who claims to be the friend of Christ. He preaches

THE DOCTRINE OF DEVILS

in the pulpit, he writes learned books, he publishes articles in the religious magazines. He attacks Christianity from within. He makes the church and the school a lodging place for every unclean and hateful bird. He leavens the meal with the doctrine of the Sadducees."[12] Peter told us these false teachers "will secretly introduce destructive heresies." Secretly means covertly, to bring in by the side of, or alongside. Paul refers to the same concept when he writes about "false believers [who] had infiltrated our ranks to spy on the freedom we have in Christ Jesus and to make us slaves" (Gal. 2:4). Moreover, Jude speaks of "certain individuals whose condemnation was written about long ago have secretly slipped in among you. They are ungodly people, who pervert the grace of our God into a license for immorality and deny Jesus Christ our only Sovereign and Lord" (Jude 4). The false prophets will present error right next to the truth by adding their doctrine alongside historical truths of Christianity. They will submit their own opinion in the place of truth and allow a mixture in the teachings to cause the undiscerning to fall for unscrupulous doctrines.

The teachers Peter, Paul, and Jude warn us about are skilled, yet they deal in an underhanded way. According to Warren Wiersbe, "They use our vocabulary but not our dictionary."[13] In other words, they have the right terminology with the wrong definitions. Their teaching is destructive, even damnable. The Greek word for destructive is *apoleia*. It is used eighteen times in the New Testament, and five of those times the word occurs in the second Epistle of Peter. Something that is destructive is ruinous. In the context of Peter's writing, *apoleia* causes a loss of well-being and eternal separation from God. Indeed, it is a destruction consisting of eternal misery in hell. In light of the series of warnings Christ and His apostles deliver to us about false prophets, no wonder Satan and his emissaries are so actively persistent in seducing church leaders. It is imperative they work while they can still dupe people in the church and place their lives on the highway to eternal misery.

APOSTASY

We need to examine the term *apostasy*, for many unbiblical views concerning it are circulating among us. Many are teaching that an apostate is

---

12. W. A. Criswell, *Believer's Study Bible: New King James Version* (Nashville: Thomas Nelson, 1991).
13. Warren W. Wierbe, *Be Alert* (Colorado Springs: David C. Cook, 2010).

THE UTOPIA OF A STRANGE LOVE

someone who was never saved in the first place. The verse that's frequently used to support this view is 1 John 2:19. Instead of using this verse to paint a broad brush, let's examine this verse contextually to get the precise meaning. In this Epistle, the apostle John was confronting the heresy of Gnosticism, which was spreading throughout the churches in Asia Minor. Gnosticism is derived from the Greek word *gnosis*, meaning to know, or knowledge. Those who taught it believed that salvation could only be gained through a secret knowledge, and only the elite had privilege to this mystical knowledge.

Among other diabolical things they believed, they taught that Jesus only "appeared" to have human form but that He was actually Spirit only. They also taught that His divine Spirit came upon His body at baptism and departed before His crucifixion. These heretical views were a frontal assault on the gospel—not only to destroy the true humanity of Christ but also His atonement. John challenged these views in 1:1-4, 4:2-3, and 5:6. If someone does not believe in the incarnation of Christ, His deity, and His atonement on the cross, it is clear that this person could not be saved, even though they are "in" the church.

It is from this assessment that John writes, "They went out from us, but they were not of us." But this view of apostasy does not apply in every circumstance. By definition, what is an apostate? It is one who defects from the truth. It is one who abandons a previous loyalty or one who renounces—falls away from—the faith. God called Israel an apostate nation because they had turned away from walking in the right paths. Some believers, in the book of Galatians, were on the threshold of deserting the true gospel for another gospel (Gal. 1:6-9). An example of someone who became an apostate was Demas. In his brief letter to Philemon, Paul wrote, "Epaphras, my fellow prisoner in Christ Jesus, sends you greetings. And so do Mark, Aristarchus, Demas and Luke, my fellow workers" (Philem. 23-24). Demas was obviously a believer, as Paul called him a fellow worker [in Christ]. However, in his second letter to Timothy, Paul reveals that Demas deserted him: "Do your best to come to me quickly, for Demas, because he loved this world, has deserted me and has gone to Thessalonica" (2 Tim. 4:9-10). Demas clearly worked for the Lord and walked on the right path, but the love of the world turned his heart, and he abandoned Paul and the gospel. He had apostatized—fallen away—and one cannot fall away from something one never possessed or from something that was never real.

THE DOCTRINE OF DEVILS

Another term for apostasy is the word *AWOL* (absent without leave). In military terminology, it means desertion, to abandon a duty or post without permission. Serious punishments are brought upon soldiers who forsake their mission, yet, one must think, how can one be charged for AWOL but never have enlisted and been sworn in for service? Those who fall away from the truth will bring upon themselves swift destruction. The false teacher's persistent denial of the Master will initiate a process of judgment that can come at any moment. When it does come, it will end in a loss of eternal life.

Satan's agenda in promoting the doctrine of devils in the church is not to teach about demons but to seduce the minds of those who have gained influence within the body of Christ. Peter makes it clear that "many will follow their evil teaching and shameful immorality. And because of these teachers, the way of truth will be slandered" (2 Pet. 2:2). Many will fall into the same destructive ways as the fraudulent teachers. The enemy's objective is not necessarily to attack the average Christian but to seduce the Christian leader. With the leader in hand, he can infiltrate the rest of the body of Christ. Moreover, Satan is not using unnamed men and women to deceive many. He uses popular leaders, some of whom ascend to great heights in the church. People follow them based on their high profile, their winning personalities, and their obvious abilities. It is true that the people of God are a product of who they follow! We cannot partake of error and be OK with Christ.

The church would be in better shape by far if we defended Christ and His Word the way we defend some of our favorite preachers, many of whom are apostates. Too many in the church today are fans of men and not so much fans of Jesus. In America, we are a celebrity-driven culture, and that same mindset has made its way into the church. It is a sad thing to say, but while many church people are divided over personalities, few are divided over bad teachings. Many lying prophets in the church today are declared righteous and holy by their notoriety and uniqueness and not by their soundness. How have they become accepted and followed? It is because they appear righteous and holy. But Jesus said, "Watch out for false prophets. They come to you in sheep's clothing, but inwardly they are ferocious wolves" (Matt. 7:15).

Some of us are so overwhelmed by the outer appearance of disingenuous prophets that our minds become numb to the poison they

THE UTOPIA OF A STRANGE LOVE

spew. I once heard a story about how the Sioux Indians caught buffaloes. When hunting buffaloes, the Sioux learned not to approach the herd directly, for then they would run out of range of their spears. After many unsuccessful attempts, they came upon a plan that eventually worked with ease. The hunters wrapped themselves in the skin of an animal the buffaloes did not fear. Closer and closer they edged up to the unsuspecting herd. When close enough, they ripped off the animal skin and speared the buffalo in the heart.

    This is tantamount to the strategy of Satan and his ministers who "come to you in sheep's clothing, but inwardly they are ferocious wolves." Sheep are fearful animals that run when they see wolves. Deadly teachers wrap themselves in sheep's clothing so they do not appear dangerous to the flock. They refrain from preaching or teaching on alarming subjects. They rarely preach "doom and gloom," but they do teach on encouragement. They usually stay away from divisive doctrines in order to emphasize themes of unity, purpose, and personal goals. Eternal judgement, the wrath of God, and repentance are topics they almost never broach—but they do teach forgiveness. As the sheep slowly embrace these friendly, non-threatening teachers, Satan draws in closer to drive a dagger into the heart.

    One dagger is the unbiblical view of the love God.

WHEN HISTORY REPEATS ITSELF

Not long ago I watched the anniversary coverage of the Jonestown Massacre, where over nine hundred people lost their lives under the direction of cult leader Jim Jones. One particular scene that caught my attention was horrific but was at the same time somewhat cryptic. A photo showed the many deceased bodies spread out around Jones and his concocted makeshift "throne." A huge sign hung on top of the throne that read, *Those who cannot remember the past are condemned to repeat it.*

What a compelling and prophetic warning. This was a quote from the Spanish philosopher George Santayana from his The Life of Reason (1905). These words speak to the situation the church finds itself in today. We have become silent to our history. We quote the words of Solomon: "What has been will be again, what has been done will be done again; there is nothing new under the sun" (Eccles. 1:9). However, as English evangelist Leonard Ravenhill said, "The one thing we learn from history is that we don't learn from history."[14] C. S. Lewis reminds us that one of Satan's ploys is to keep us from discerning what appears to be new. He called it "the great cataract of nonsense," the tendency to concern ourselves with the present while divorcing ourselves from history, therefore becoming blind to the knowledge of earlier times.[15]

If history really repeats itself, why do we believe current teachings that in times past were condemned by the church as heretical? Why are we accepting things that God rejected long ago? The church ignores its history at its own peril. A lack of historical perspective from the pulpit proves that what Bible teacher Howard Hendricks once said is true: "A mist in the pulpit is a fog in the pews."[16] Any pastor or Christian leader who slights the lessons

---

14. Leonard Ravenhill, *Why Revival Tarries: A Classic on Revival.*
15. C. S. Lewis, "Learning In War-Time," October 22, 1939, message from C. S. Lewis website.
16. Source unknown.

THE UTOPIA OF A STRANGE LOVE

from church history cannot be God's present voice. Why? Being blind to the past makes one a target to deceiving spirits that will introduce revelations and insights appearing fresh and relevant but which are heretical. It is shameful that the body of Christ supports teachings the apostles would have considered the workings of evil.

When God rejected Saul as king, the prophet Samuel was ordered to go to Jesse's house to anoint God's chosen one. Here is the story from 1 Samuel 16:1-7:

> The Lord said to Samuel, "How long will you mourn for Saul, since I have rejected him as king over Israel? Fill your horn with oil and be on your way; I am sending you to Jesse of Bethlehem. I have chosen one of his sons to be king." But Samuel said, "How can I go? If Saul hears about it, he will kill me." The Lord said, "Take a heifer with you and say, 'I have come to sacrifice to the LORD.' Invite Jesse to the sacrifice, and I will show you what to do. You are to anoint for me the one I indicate." Samuel did what the Lord said. When he arrived at Bethlehem, the elders of the town trembled when they met him. They asked, "Do you come in peace?" Samuel replied, "Yes, in peace; I have come to sacrifice to the Lord. Consecrate yourselves and come to the sacrifice with me." Then he consecrated Jesse and his sons and invited them to the sacrifice. When they arrived, Samuel saw Eliab and thought, "Surely the Lord's anointed stands here before the Lord." But the Lord said to Samuel, "Do not consider his appearance or his height, for I have rejected him. The Lord does not look at the things people look at. People look at the outward appearance, but the Lord looks at the heart."

When Samuel saw Jesse's oldest son, Eliab, he immediately tried to anoint him. Yet God spoke and said Eliab was not the one. What made Samuel assume Eliab was to be the next king? Because he looked like the former king. He had the bearing and the looks but not the approval. Samuel almost fell into the human tendency to accept things God previously rejected.

We live in a visually driven culture. We have worked so hard to become relevant to a passing culture that we are on the precipice of becoming completely detached from the voice of history. A. W. Tozer, an American pastor and author, said, "Not wanting to appear judgmental we mistakenly try to make biblical truth fit the culture around us."[17] We are not led by the Spirit of God; we are led by our feelings, opinions, and eyes. When a generation starts listening with their eyes, they will eventually become hard of hearing, and when the church turns her back on the past, she will embrace false representatives teaching delusional doctrines. One such person from history was a bishop named Marcion of Sinope (85–160 AD). As we uncover his teaching, which forced the early church fathers to condemn and excommunicate him, we will find that it has been revived and repackaged today. It shows that we as a church too often welcome reinvented lies.

Marcionism

Several decades after the apostle John passed away, a bishop named Marcion began teaching a doctrine that led many astray and nearly divided the church. Marcion thought the teachings of Jesus were incompatible with what he saw of the God of the Old Testament, and consequently he rejected the God of the Hebrew scriptures. He taught that the God of the New Testament is a different God from the God of the Old Testament. These different deities accounted for the contradictions between Old Covenant theology and gospel theology. Marcion developed the idea of two Gods, a lower one (the God of the Old Testament) and a higher, more transcendent one (the God of Jesus in the New Testament).

Tertullian (155–240 AD) was a Christian author and apologist from Carthage in North Africa who had this to say about Marcion:

> Marcion has quenched the light of his faith, and so lost the God whom he had found. His disciples will not deny that his first faith he held along with ourselves; a letter of his own proves this; so that for the future heretic may from his case be designated as one who, forsaking that which was prior, afterwards chose out for himself that which was not in times past. For in as far as what was delivered in times past and from the beginning will be held as truth, in so far will that be accounted heresy, which is brought in later. But another brief treatise will maintain this position against heretics, who ought to be refuted even without a consideration of their doctrines, on the ground that they are heretical by reason of

---

17. A. W. Tozer and James L. Snyder, *God's Power for Your Life: How the Holy Spirit Transforms You Through God's Word* (Bloomington, MN: Bethany House, 2013).

THE UTOPIA OF A STRANGE LOVE

the novelty of their opinions. Now, so far as any controversy is to be admitted, I will for the time (lest our compendious principle of novelty, being called in on all occasions to our aid, should be imputed to want of confidence) begin with setting forth our adversary's rule of belief, that it may escape no one what our main contention is to be.[18] In the first place, how arrogantly do the Marcionites build up their stupid system, bringing forward a new god, as if we were ashamed of the old one![19] Listen, ye sinners; and ye who have not yet come to this, hear, that you may attain to such a pass! A better god has been discovered, who never takes offence, is never angry, never inflicts punishment, who has prepared no fire in hell, no gnashing of teeth in the outer darkness! He is purely and simply good. He indeed forbids all delinquency, but only in word. He is in you, if you are willing to pay him homage, for the sake of appearances, that you may seem to honour God; for your fear he does not want. And so satisfied are the Marcionites with such pretenses, that they have no fear of their god at all. They say it is only a bad man who will be feared, a good man will be loved. Foolish man, do you say that he whom you call Lord ought not to be feared, whilst the very title you give him indicates a power which must itself be feared? But how are you going to love, without some fear that you do not love? Surely (such a god) is neither your Father, towards whom your love for duty's sake should be consistent with fear because of His power; nor your proper Lord, whom you should love for His humanity and fear as your teacher.[20]

Irenaeus (early 2nd century–c. 202 AD) was Bishop of Lugdunum in Gaul, which was then part of the Roman Empire and is now Lyon, France. Irenaeus was an apologist who wrote against early heresies of the church. He wrote this in connection to Marcion:

---

18. *Ante-Nicene Fathers: The Writings of the Fathers down to A.D. 325*, ed. Alexander Roberts and James Donaldson. Revised and chronologically arranged with brief prefaces and occasional notes by A. Cleveland Coxe (New York: Christian Literature Publishing Co., 1885). Public domain.
19. Quintus Tertullian and Paul A. Boer Sr., "The Anti-Marcion Writings of Tertullian" (Seattle: CreateSpace Independent Publishing Platform, 2012).
20. Tertullian, *Against Marcion*, Vol. 3 (Ante-Nicene Fathers 3:292).

WHEN HISTORY REPEATS ITSELF

Cerdo was one who took his system from the followers of Simon, and came to live at Rome in the time of Hyginus, who held the ninth place in the episcopal succession from the apostles downwards. He taught that the God proclaimed by the law and the prophets was not the Father of our Lord Jesus Christ. For the former was known, but the latter unknown; while the one also was righteous, but the other benevolent. Marcion of Pontus succeeded him, and developed his doctrine. In so doing, he advanced the most daring blasphemy against Him who is proclaimed as God by the law and the prophets, declaring Him to be the author of evils, to take delight in war, to be infirm of purpose, and even to be contrary to Himself. But Jesus being derived from that father who is above the God that made the world, and coming into Judea in the times of Pontius Pilate the governor, who was the procurator of Tiberius Caesar, was manifested in the form of a man to those who were in Judea, abolishing the prophets and the law, and all the works of that God who made the world, whom also he calls Cosmocrator. Besides this, he mutilates the Gospel which is according to Luke, removing all that is written respecting the generation of the Lord, and setting aside a great deal of the teaching of the Lord, in which the Lord is recorded as most clearly confessing that the Maker of this universe is His Father. He likewise persuaded his disciples that he himself was more worthy of credit than are those apostles who have handed down the Gospel to us, furnishing them not with the Gospel, but merely a fragment of it. In like manner, too, he dismembered the Epistles of Paul, removing all that is said by the apostle respecting that God who made the world, to the effect that He is the Father of our Lord Jesus Christ, and also those passages from the prophetical writings which the apostle quotes, in order to teach us that they announced beforehand the coming of the Lord. Salvation will be the attainment only of those souls which had learned his doctrine; while the body, as having been taken from the earth, is incapable of sharing in salvation. In addition to his blasphemy against God Himself, he advanced this also, truly speaking as with the mouth of the devil, and saying all things in direct opposition to the truth,—that Cain, and those like him, and the Sodomites, and the Egyptians, and others like them, and, in fine, all the nations who walked in all sorts of abomination, were saved by the Lord, on His descending into Hades, and on their running unto Him, and that they welcomed Him into their kingdom. But the serpent which

THE UTOPIA OF A STRANGE LOVE

was in Marcion declared that Abel, and Enoch, and Noah, and those other righteous men who sprang from the patriarch Abraham, with all the prophets, and those who were pleasing to God, did not partake in salvation. For since these men, he says, knew that their God was constantly tempting them, so now they suspected that He was tempting them, and did not run to Jesus, or believe His announcement: and for this reason he declared that their souls remained in Hades. But since this man is the only one who has dared openly to mutilate the Scriptures, and unblushingly above all others to inveigh against God, I purpose specially to refute him, convicting him out of his own writings; and, with the help of God, I shall overthrow him out of those discourses of the Lord and the apostles, which are of authority with him, and of which he makes use. At present, however, I have simply been led to mention him, that thou mightest know that all those who in any way corrupt the truth, and injuriously affect the preaching of the Church, are the disciples and successors of Simon Magus of Samaria. Although they do not confess the name of their master, in order all the more to seduce others, yet they do teach his doctrines. They set forth, indeed, the name of Christ Jesus as a sort of lure, but in various ways they introduce the impieties of Simon; and thus they destroy multitudes, wickedly disseminating their own doctrines by the use of a good name, and, through means of its sweetness and beauty, extending to their hearers the bitter and malignant poison of the serpent, the great author of apostasy.[21]

Justin Martyr (100–165 AD), also known as Saint Justin, was another early apologist who introduced the idea of the Logos to the early church. He said that the demonstration of the Word acting in the world could be identified even before the inauguration of Christianity. Saint Justin wrote this about Marcion:

And there is Marcion a man of Pontus, who is even at this day alive, and teaching his disciples to believe in some other god greater than the Creator. And he, by the aid of the devils, has caused many of every nation to speak blasphemies, and to deny that God is the maker of this universe, and to assert

---

21. Saint Irenaeus, *Against Heresies*, Complete, by New Advent (online content), Vol. 1, chapter 27, www.newadvent.org/fathers/03121.htm.

that some other being, greater than He, has done greater works. All who take their opinions from these men, are, as we before said, called Christians.[22]

With the insight of Tertullian, Irenaeus, and Justin Martyr, we can develop a clear picture of Marcion's beliefs. He was a true follower of Christ in the beginning, but later, seduced by Satan, he became an apostate. What did he teach? He taught that the New Testament gives us a picture of a better God than we see in the Hebrew scriptures. The God of the New Testament was different from the one in the Old Testament. This "better God" had nothing to do with wrath, law, and judgment, such as we see in the older testament, but was instead a God of, mercy, love, and grace. Marcion taught a dualistic system where the two Gods are separate and the opposite of each other. He taught that the Old Testament deity was not the God and Father of Jesus Christ. The God of the Old Testament was the God of Creation, but He was a harsh master, cruel, and incompetent. Marcion contrasted this creating God with the God of Jesus, who was loving and forgiving. Marcion violently repudiated the subject of judgment, found so often in the Old Testament, while he approved of the message of grace and love in the New Testament. Once again, for Marcion,

- The God of the Old Testament is not the God of the New Testament.
- The God of the Old Testament is unjust, vindictive, angry, and harsh.
- The God of the New Testament represents grace, forgiveness, and love.
- The God of the New Testament does not judge and does not punish believers.
- Except for Paul, who preached grace, all the apostles preached the law.

---

22. Justin Martyr, *First Apology* 27 (ANF, 1:171).

THE UTOPIA OF A STRANGE LOVE

- Paul is the only apostle we should listen to because he had the true message for the church.

- Any message on judgment and repentance represents the Old Testament God.

- Even Jesus' Sermon on the Mount message is to be avoided because it is law.

- The law and grace are totally opposite of one another, with grace being superior.

- The God of the New Testament had been unknown until revealed in Jesus Christ. This new God is a higher God than the old. This new God has only love, and is incapable of condemning anyone.

- Jesus sees only our goodness, not our sins.

- The only message for today's church should be grace and love.

Does Marcion's doctrine ring any bells? Today, some of the most active churches and charismatic leaders are those who teach a distorted message of love and grace that originated with Marcion. They proclaim a damnable heresy that repentance and judgment are not for believers! Marcion himself drew the sort of crowds many pastors today would love to attract. How could he not only get away with but succeed in attracting so many other believers with such diabolical views? The apostle Paul's warning gives us an indicator:

> Keep watch over yourselves and all the flock of which the Holy Spirit has made you overseers. Be shepherds of the church of God, which he bought with his own blood. I know that after I leave, savage wolves will come in among you and will not spare the flock. Even from your own number men will arise and distort the truth in order to draw away disciples after them. So be on your guard! Remember that for three years I never stopped warning each of you night and day with tears. (Acts 20:28-31)

WHEN HISTORY REPEATS ITSELF

Paul predicted that men would rise from within the church and distort the scriptures, all with the intention of drawing people after themselves. Marcion convinced believers to abandon original Christian teachings that were over a century old. That took not only intellectual stamina but, more to the point, the influence of seducing spirits. Pastor and author John MacArthur has written that "False teaching does not come from the creativity of men, but from demons."[23] How did Marcion persuade Christians, who relied upon and trusted the sacredness of the Old Testament, to reject its documents and message? He created his own doctrine! He took scissors to the Bible and removed the whole Hebrew testament. He also removed the books of Matthew, Mark, and John. He kept the Gospel of Luke, but he removed the first four chapters of it.[24] Because Paul, with his focus on grace, was Marcion's favorite apostle, he rejected the writings attributed to all the other apostles and relied on ten of Paul's letters.

John Knox (1513–1572) was a Scottish clergyman and one of the leaders of the Protestant Reformation. He wrote . . .

> . . . that Marcion, for example, did not have the account of John the Baptist's announcement of Jesus as Messiah or the story of Jesus' temptation is almost certainly to be accounted for by Marcion's omission of these passages. Not only are they inconsistent with Marcion's theological position but (more important) they are also deeply imbedded in the Synoptic tradition, and to explain them as late additions to a Gospel which was already dependent (as Marcion's was) upon that tradition is next to impossible.[25]

New Testament scholar F. F. Bruce said, "Marcion dealt with the text of Paul's letters in the same way as with the text of Luke's gospel: anything which appeared inconsistent with what he believed to be authentic Pauline teaching was regarded as a corruption proceeding from an alien hand."[26] Tertullian certainly agreed: "Of the scriptures we have our being before there was any other way, before they were interpolated by [heretics].

---

23. John MacArthur, "Understanding The Seducing Spirit," August 31, 1986, message from Grace To You website.
24. F. F. Bruce, *The Canon of Scripture* (Downers Grove, IL: InterVarsity, 1998), 134-144.
25. John Knox, *Marcion and the New Testament* (Chicago: University of Chicago, 1942), 95.
26. Bruce, *The Canon of Scripture*, 140.

THE UTOPIA OF A STRANGE LOVE

... One man perverts the scriptures with his hand, another their meaning by his exposition. Marcion expressly and openly used the knife, not the pen, since he made such an excision of the scriptures as suited his own subject-matter."[27]

Joseph Prince

Is history repeating itself? I am going to offer some direct quotes from one of the leading "grace teachers" active in the church today. His name is Joseph Prince, and he is the senior pastor of New Creation Church in Singapore, which is one of Asia's biggest churches. His teaching is almost entirely heterodox, but his popularity, power, and influence impacts not only those in the pews but those in the pulpits. In fact, his message on grace has become a template for many leaders. What does he teach?

> Under the new covenant, we don't have to keep on asking the Lord for forgiveness because he has already forgiven us.[28]

> For the law was given by Moses, but grace and truth came by Jesus Christ. Have you noticed that truth is on the side of grace, not the law?[29]

> I distinctly heard the voice of the Lord on the inside. It wasn't a witness of the Spirit. It was a voice, and I heard God say this clearly to me: "Son, you are not preaching grace." I said, "What do you mean, Lord...." "Every time you preach grace, you preach it with a mixture of law. You attempt to balance grace with the law like many other preachers, and the moment you balance grace, you neutralize it. You cannot put new wine into old wineskins. You cannot put grace and law together." He went on to say, "Son, a lot of preachers are not preaching grace the way Apostle Paul preached grace."[30]

---

27. Tertullian, *Against Marcion* 38 (ANF, 3:262).
28. Joseph Prince, *Destined to Reign: The Secret to Effortless Success, Wholeness, and Victorious Living* (Tulsa: Harrison House, 2007), 7.
29. Ibid., 12.
30. Ibid., vii.

WHEN HISTORY REPEATS ITSELF

Grace is personal and came as a person—the person of Jesus Christ. The law is hard, cold and impersonal. You cannot have a relationship with two pieces of stone. But grace is gentle and warm. Grace is not a teaching or doctrine. Grace is a person and you can have a relationship with a person.[31]

My friend, those who believe that God is sometimes angry with them are still living under the old covenant of the law and not under the new covenant of grace.[32]

I have also heard some believers pronouncing, "If God does not judge America for all its sins, God has to apologize to Sodom and Gomorrah." Well, let me say this with honor and respect: If God judges America today, He has to apologize to Jesus and what He has accomplished on the cross! My friend, God is not judging America (or any country in the world today).[33]

You will never find an example of God punishing a believer for his sins in the new covenant.[34]

You see, faith does not come by simply hearing the word of God because the word of God would encompass everything in the Bible, including the Law of Moses. There is no impartation of faith when you hear the Ten Commandments preached. Faith only comes by hearing the word of Christ . . . Only when Christ is preached will faith be imparted.[35]

Some of the words which Jesus spoke in the four gospels . . . are part of the old covenant. They were spoken before the cross as He had not yet died. The new covenant only

---

31. Ibid., 12.
32. Ibid., 38.
33. Ibid., 49.
34. Ibid., 57.
35. Ibid., 75.

THE UTOPIA OF A STRANGE LOVE

begins after the cross, when the Holy Spirit was given on the day of Pentecost.[36]

Not everything that Jesus said was spoken to the church. Paul's letters were written to the church and are thus for our benefit today. God raised him up to write the words of the ascended Jesus . . . That is why, when it comes to reading the Bible, I always encourage new believers in our church to begin with the letters of Paul. (Many new believers like to start with the book of Revelation or Genesis, without first getting a foundation in the gospel of grace through reading the letters of Paul.)[37]

Listen carefully: We don't have to confess our sins in order to be forgiven. We confess our sins because we are already forgiven . . . I'm talking about being open with God . . . So confession in the new covenant is just being honest about your failures and your humanity. It is the result of being forgiven and not something you do in order to be forgiven.[38]

I took 1 John 1:9 ["If we confess our sins, he is faithful and just and will forgive us our sins and purify us from all unrighteousness"] to the limit and it nearly drove me insane. But what does 1 John 1:9 really say and to whom was it actually written . . . People have actually taken this verse and built a whole doctrine around it when in actuality, chapter 1 of 1 John was written to the Gnostics, who were unbelievers.[39]

The Bible says that "The goodness of God leads you to repentance." . . . Nevertheless, there are still people who insist that we have to preach on repentance. Well, I disagree!

---

36. Ibid., 92.
37. Ibid., 94.
38. Ibid., 104.
39. Ibid., 106.

I think that we should do it God's way—preach the goodness of God to lead people to repentance.[40]

These are only some of the distorted and unorthodox comments made by this leader. It is shocking that a single book can obtain such unmitigated error, yet his book became a best seller and helped create a huge following for the author. Is there any similarity between the beliefs of Marcion and Joseph Prince? Yes. Both teach that what Jesus taught was incompatible with the teaching of the Hebrew scriptures, and both reject the inspiration of and the God of the Old Testament. How could the early church excommunicate Marcion as a heretic when today's church embraces and creates platforms for Prince as God-sent? This was the early church diagnosis of Marcion:

> To any church leader, Marcion's heresy was the most shocking deviation from Apostolic truth. He had denied the Old Testament's inspiration and the continuity of the God and Creator with Christ. Bishop Polycarp had known how to deal with him. When Polycarp met Marcion, said Polycarp's pupil Irenaeus, he had greeted him as "the first born child of Satan."[41]

If Polycarp lived today, one can imagine critics calling him judgmental, overly critical, graceless, and unloving. Yet how loving is it not to call heresy by its name? What has happened to the church? Why does the church try so hard to win the world's approval with false teaching on God's love when the church's Messiah and Savior said specifically, "You will be hated by everyone because of me, but the one who stands firm to the end will be saved" (Matt. 10:22)? Are we offended and ashamed by the hard truths in the Word of God?

In his book *The Pilgrim Church*, Christian missionary Edmund Hamer Broadbent (1861–1945) states that "Any error may be founded on parts of Scripture; the truth alone is based on the whole. Marcion's errors were the inevitable result of his accepting only what pleased him and rejecting the

---

40. Ibid., 231-232.
41. Robin Lane Fox, *Pagans and Christians* (London: Penguin Books Limited, 2006), 492.

THE UTOPIA OF A STRANGE LOVE

rest."[42] The same comment can be made of Joseph Prince. God spoke of a time coming when the church would not endure wholesome and sound teaching:

> For the time will come when people will not put up with sound doctrine. Instead, to suit their own desires, they will gather around them a great number of teachers to say what their itching ears want to hear. They will turn their ears away from the truth and turn aside to myths. (2 Tim. 4:3-4)

Men turning their ears from the truth and pursuing made-up beliefs is what we see in the phenomenon of so-called "grace teachers" like Joseph Prince. God, in His wisdom, knew that men and women would distort the doctrine of Christ, and He directed many warnings at them, including these:

> Dear friends, since you are looking forward to this, make every effort to be found spotless, blameless and at peace with him. Bear in mind that our Lord's patience means salvation, just as our dear brother Paul also wrote you with the wisdom that God gave him. He writes the same way in all his letters, speaking in them of these matters. His letters contain some things that are hard to understand, which ignorant and unstable people distort, as they do the other Scriptures, to their own destruction. Therefore, dear friends, since you have been forewarned, be on your guard so that you may not be carried away by the error of the lawless and fall from your secure position. But grow in the grace and knowledge of our Lord and Savior Jesus Christ. To him be glory both now and forever! Amen. (2 Pet. 3:14-18)

> Anyone who runs ahead and does not continue in the teaching of Christ does not have God; whoever continues in the teaching has both the Father and the Son. If anyone comes to you and does not bring this teaching, do not take

---

42. E. H. Broadbent, *The Pilgrim Church*, 2nd edition (London: Pickering & Inglis, 1935), 15.

them into your house or welcome them. Anyone who welcomes them shares in their wicked work. (2 John 9-11)

The church needs to wake up, because a distorted message of grace is usurping and perverting the proper understanding of God's love. The enemy is keeping us blind and ignorant to our own history, for he knows those who will not remember the past are destined to repeat it.

THE SECRET MEETING

Many tender-minded Christians fear to sin against love by daring to inquire into anything that comes wearing the cloak of Christianity and breathing the name of Jesus. They dare not examine the credentials of the latest prophet to hit their town lest they be guilty of rejecting something which may be of God. They timidly remember how the Pharisees refused to accept Christ when He came, and they do not want to be caught in the same snare, so they either reserve judgment or shut their eyes and accept everything without question. This is supposed to indicate a high degree of spirituality. But in sober fact it indicates no such thing. It may indeed be evidence of the absence of the Holy Spirit. Gullibility is not synonymous with spirituality. . . . *Try the spirits* is a command of the Holy Spirit to the Church. We may sin as certainly by approving the spurious as by rejecting the genuine. And the current habit of refusing to take sides is not the way to avoid the question. To appraise things with a heart of love and then to act on the results is an obligation resting upon every Christian in the world. And the more as we see the day approaching.[43]

Seventeenth century English philosopher and physician John Locke has been credited with saying, "Whoever defines the word, defines the world."[44] In hindsight, Locke was speaking prophetically, not only to the culture but also to the church. The modern church is in the habit of redefining words in an attempt to please the culture. Often the church does not redefine words so much as embrace outright worldly definitions of words. It has done this because it has allowed the world to force it to jettison the Bible and believe their way. A perfect example of this is the word *love*, which has been hijacked and sold for ransom to today's Christians. Paul told Timothy, "The

---

43. A. W. Tozer, *The Set of The Sail* (Camp Hill, PA: Wingspread, 2007), chapter 6.
44. Source unknown.

THE UTOPIA OF A STRANGE LOVE

time will come when people will not put up with sound doctrine. Instead, to suit their own desires, they will gather around them a great number of teachers to say what their itching ears want to hear. They will turn their ears away from the truth and turn aside to myths" (2 Tim. 4:3-4).

Perilous times have arrived in the church. This is not because of famine or poverty. It is not because of persecution, even though many Christian brothers and sisters around the world face this terrible challenge. No, "There will be terrible times in the last days. People will be lovers of themselves, lovers of money, boastful, proud, abusive, disobedient to their parents, ungrateful, unholy, without love, unforgiving, slanderous, without self-control, brutal, not lovers of the good" (2 Tim. 3:1-3). The word *love*, in the hands of a generation famous for the love of self, can take a deadly turn.

When the scriptures depict Satan as "the ruler of the kingdom of the air, the spirit who is now at work in those who are disobedient" (Eph. 2:2) and "the prince of this world" (John 12:31), it is noting the enemy's influencing power. But the Bible never says Satan has absolute authority. Despite popular but heretical modern-day teaching that God does not have final power and control over the earth and that God even needs human approval to work in the world, the power and rule of God is unmatched. No person can restrain His hand:

> Lord, the God of our ancestors, are you not the God who is in heaven? You rule over all the kingdoms of the nations. Power and might are in your hand, and no one can withstand you. (2 Chron. 20:6)

> The Lord has established his throne in heaven, and his kingdom rules over all. (Ps. 103:19)

> At the end of that time, I, Nebuchadnezzar, raised my eyes toward heaven, and my sanity was restored. Then I praised the Most High; I honored and glorified him who lives forever. His dominion is an eternal dominion; his kingdom endures from generation to generation. All the peoples of the earth are regarded as nothing. He does as he pleases with the powers of heaven and the peoples of the earth. No one can hold back his hand or say to him: "What have you done?" (Dan. 4:335)

Love or Tolerance?

In His sovereignty, God has allowed Satan to operate within strict boundaries. Satan's role in influencing unbiblical thoughts, opinions, ideas, goals, views, and beliefs into the minds of humankind is a major one. His influencing power, coupled with human selfishness, is a tool that leads untold numbers to miss the narrow gate, "For wide is the gate and broad is the road that leads to destruction, and many enter through it" (Matt. 7:13). One way we miss the narrow gate is when we redefine love as tolerance, as suggested earlier. Excessive tolerance—in the name of love—causes Christians to drop biblical standards in an effort to be accepted by the world. But this is conformity, not love.

It is common to hear such phrases floating around the church as, "God just wants me to love, period," "We have to love more and stop letting doctrine divide us," "Jesus just loved people; He wasn't too concerned about their beliefs," and "Love over doctrine is how we will draw the world to us." This attitude has become the accepted mindset, and an undue concern over doctrinal things will get one labeled unloving, critical, judgmental, negative, and out of step with a society given over to tolerance as the fundamental moral and personal value. Once the dross is stripped away, however—once we get to the root of such thinking—it becomes clear that this value has nothing to do with love from a biblical point of view. It is just human-centered sentimentalism, a human attempt to reach nonbelievers by intuition. In the attempt, however, God's Word is suppressed, His way to salvation is rejected, and countless are led to believe without scriptural support that God's love is protecting them. How did the church get to this point? How did she allow the culture's view of *love* to become supreme? How did doctrine become the bad guy?

Love God, Love People

Several years ago, George Barna, a market researcher who studies the religious beliefs of Americans, conducted a poll showing that Christians and non-Christians alike thought Christians were too judgmental, hypocritical, dogmatic, and unloving.[45] Some young and innovative pastors came

---

45. David Kinnaman and Gabe Lyons, *unChristian: What a New Generation Really Thinks about Christianity . . . and Why It Matters* (Grand Rapids: Baker Books, 2007), 33-34. Presented

THE UTOPIA OF A STRANGE LOVE

together to see how they could reverse this preconception and make Christianity seem more relevant to the culture. They did this outside of the observation of their congregations. What did this secret meeting produce?

Throughout the country, churches began changing their names to something that lacked any denominational identification and that had a more relevant and bold tone. They removed parts of the service that seemed in line with traditional or historical Christianity. Surveys were conducted to the surrounding communities to find out what they wanted to see and hear in church. Some believed that this ideal was very good. But what also came of these surveys was destructive—a removal of doctrine and expositional Bible teaching and preaching. There was an overwhelming zeal on the part of some of these pastors to distance themselves from hard and unpopular teachings in the Bible and the "narrow-minded" beliefs that made some Christians seem unloving. They seemed to forget that Paul told us to "watch your life and doctrine closely. Persevere in them, because if you do, you will save both yourself and your hearers" (1 Tim. 4:16), and "You . . . must teach what is appropriate to sound doctrine" (Titus 2:1). Only sound doctrine can build spiritual maturity, character, and strength.

The old approach was no longer tolerable, so out with hard Bible doctrines and in with soft subjects concerning felt needs, self-worth, maximizing potential, feeling significant, reaching one's goals in life, and finding purpose. They introduced elements of mysticism. They emphasized dialog and the developing nature of the church. They were disillusioned with the organized church and wanted to deconstruct worship, evangelism, and the Christian community. Formats emphasizing salvation were abandoned.

---

in this book is a poll conducted by George Barna, which revealed that "four out of five young churchgoers say that Christianity is anti-homosexual; half describe it as judgmental, too involved in politics, hypocritical, and confusing; one-third believe their faith is old-fashioned and out of touch with reality; and one-quarter of young Christians believe it is boring and insensitive to others." Those outside the church hold increasingly negative views of Christians as well. Among young people (aged 16-29), roughly 49 percent hold an "extraordinarily negative" view of evangelical Christians and only 3 percent have a "good" impression. The authors reached a conclusion that this younger generation of Christians is simply and rightfully frustrated by the fact that this very real condition serves to inhibit their efforts to share the love of Christ with others. In other words, contemporary American Christianity carries with it a lot of negative baggage. So much so that "they feel raising the 'Christian flag' would actually undermine their ability to connect with people and maintain credibility with them." And so, they feel they must "distance themselves from the current 'branding' of Christianity."

THE SECRET MEETING

All of this was done to appeal to the non-Christians in the midst of the church.

The alternative approach was very successful, for now the church could "minister" to those who were previously turned off by biblical mandates such as eternal punishment and penal substitution. But they were not done yet. They were looking for something more exciting. An idea was formed that would be the driving force behind the slogan, *Love God, Love People*. The new brand of the church would be called *emergent*. The new theme of the church would be *missional*.

While this sounds like the ideal purpose of the church, what the new movement produced is another gospel. This other gospel was produced from a re-engineering of the church in a rebrand of the social gospel. The social gospel is the belief that the objective of the church is to address and meet the temporal needs of man. It's a view that believes the church's primary focus should be to root out society ills. Paul addressed the question of a different gospel with the churches in Corinth and Galatia:

> I am jealous for you with a godly jealousy. I promised you to one husband, to Christ, so that I might present you as a pure virgin to him. But I am afraid that just as Eve was deceived by the serpent's cunning, your minds may somehow be led astray from your sincere and pure devotion to Christ. For if someone comes to you and preaches a Jesus other than the Jesus we preached, or if you receive a different spirit from the Spirit you received, or a different gospel from the one you accepted, you put up with it easily enough. (2 Cor. 11:2-4)

> I am astonished that you are so quickly deserting the one who called you to live in the grace of Christ and are turning to a different gospel—which is really no gospel at all. Evidently some people are throwing you into confusion and are trying to pervert the gospel of Christ. But even if we or an angel from heaven should preach a gospel other than the one we preached to you, let them be under God's curse! As we have already said, so now I say again: If anybody is preaching to you a gospel other than what you accepted, let them be under God's curse! (Gal. 1:6-9)

THE UTOPIA OF A STRANGE LOVE

In the Greek language of the New Testament, there are two different words for the adjective *another*. There is *allos*—which means another of the *same* kind. The other word is *heteron*, which means another of a *different* kind or quality. In the verses given previously, Paul uses the word *heteron* when addressing the Corinthian and Galatian churches. While *allos* and *heteron* may appear to have the same meaning, there are significant qualitative differences. The objective of the emergent movement was to reshape the church to make it more attractive and less intimidating to the world. Sadly, what they did was silence the true gospel by substituting another gospel of a different kind.

What Does *Missional* Mean?

There seems to be no clear definition of what *missional* means. On the surface, it means leaving the four walls of the church to be missionary-like in the community. Emergent churches redefine or modify the term to fit their individual situations. The idea is that we should all be missionaries in our world—and that is an excellent idea. The problem comes when people are sent out in the communities to preach the gospel when the church has supplanted true doctrine for teachings that meet people's needs.

What at first appears to be evangelistic—to attract spiritual seekers—is far from the pattern of the original fellowship of believers:

> With many other words he warned them; and he pleaded with them, "Save yourselves from this corrupt generation." Those who accepted his message were baptized, and about three thousand were added to their number that day. They devoted themselves to the apostles' teaching and to fellowship, to the breaking of bread and to prayer. Everyone was filled with awe at the many wonders and signs performed by the apostles. All the believers were together and had everything in common. They sold property and possessions to give to anyone who had need. Every day they continued to meet together in the temple courts. They broke bread in their homes and ate together with glad and sincere hearts, praising God and enjoying the favor of all the people. And the Lord added to their number daily those who were being saved. (Acts 2:40-47)

THE SECRET MEETING

What appears to be evangelistic is also far from what Jesus commanded:

> Then Jesus came to them and said, "All authority in heaven and on earth has been given to me. Therefore go and make disciples of all nations, baptizing them in the name of the Father and of the Son and of the Holy Spirit, and teaching them to obey everything I have commanded you. And surely I am with you always, to the very end of the age." (Matt. 28:18-20)

The foundation of the missional movement is to change the emphasis in the church from outward-driven evangelism with inward devotion and spiritual growth to outward-focused "evangelism" with little or no serious spiritual growth beyond being loving and kind in one's acts. The biblical function of the church and what goes on inside the church, including the teaching of doctrine, Bible study (exposition of the scriptures), and discipleship, is replaced by an emphasis on being involved in the community. There is no training on evangelizing except for showing love and concern. Missional churches have adopted a quote commonly attributed to St. Francis of Assisi: "Preach the gospel at all times—and when necessary, use words." Doing good deeds and showing the works of Christ is a wonderful thing. But is it enough? Is it biblical? Can one show enough good works or "live" the gospel?

When the Lord and His apostles reached out into the community, they preached the true gospel:

> How, then, can they call on the one they have not believed in? And how can they believe in the one of whom they have not heard? And how can they hear without someone preaching to them? And how can anyone preach unless they are sent? As it is written: "How beautiful are the feet of those who bring good news!" But not all the Israelites accepted the good news. For Isaiah says, "Lord, who has believed our message?" Consequently, faith comes from hearing the message, and the message is heard through the word about Christ. (Rom. 10:14-17)

THE UTOPIA OF A STRANGE LOVE

How can they hear without someone preaching to them? Preaching is proclaiming, telling abroad, and calling out with a clear voice. When the gospel is proclaimed from the Bible, it is not designed to make us feel good and to pamper our flesh. It is designed to show us our sinful condition and our need of the Savior: "The sun will be turned to darkness and the moon to blood before the coming of the great and glorious day of the Lord. And everyone who calls on the name of the Lord will be saved. Fellow Israelites, listen to this: Jesus of Nazareth was a man accredited by God to you by miracles, wonders and signs, which God did among you through him, as you yourselves know" (Acts 2:20-22). As A. W. Tozer once put it, "There is plenty of good news in the Bible, but there is never any flattery or back scratching. Seen one way, the Bible is a book of doom. It condemns all men as sinners and declares that the soul that sinneth shall die. Always it pronounces sentence against society before it offers mercy; and if we will not own the validity of the sentence we cannot admit the need for mercy."[46]

When the church tries meeting the needs of a community without preaching about sin and salvation, is this not a form of pride? Is it even possible to show enough good works or "live" the gospel? None of us will ever do more good works than Jesus, and He never tried showing how concerned and loving He was to win people apart from preaching repentance. The Gospels of Matthew and Mark give us the background for when Jesus began to preach:

> When Jesus heard that John had been put in prison, he withdrew to Galilee. Leaving Nazareth, he went and lived in Capernaum, which was by the lake in the area of Zebulun and Naphtali—to fulfill what was said through the prophet Isaiah: "Land of Zebulun and land of Naphtali, the Way of the Sea, beyond the Jordan, Galilee of the Gentiles—the people living in darkness have seen a great light; on those living in the land of the shadow of death a light has dawned." From that time on Jesus began to preach, "Repent, for the kingdom of heaven has come near." (Matt. 4:12-17)

---

46. A. W. Tozer, *Man-the Dwelling Place of God* (Camp Hill, PA: Wingspread Publishing, 2008).

That evening after sunset the people brought to Jesus all the sick and demon-possessed. The whole town gathered at the door, and Jesus healed many who had various diseases. He also drove out many demons, but he would not let the demons speak because they knew who he was. Very early in the morning, while it was still dark, Jesus got up, left the house and went off to a solitary place, where he prayed. Simon and his companions went to look for him, and when they found him, they exclaimed: "Everyone is looking for you!" Jesus replied, "Let us go somewhere else—to the nearby villages—so I can preach there also. That is why I have come." So he traveled throughout Galilee, preaching in their synagogues and driving out demons. (Mark 1:32-39)

John MacArthur has written that "the basic task of the church is to teach sound doctrine. It is not to give one pastor's opinion, to recite tear-jerking illustrations that play on the emotions, to raise funds, to present programs and entertainment, or to give weekly devotionals. In Titus 2:1 Paul writes, 'Speak the things which are proper for sound doctrine.' . . . Many other things are good, but they're not priorities."[47]

Another Gospel

When the pastors met to form the emergent church movement, their intentions may have been right. However, their emphases had nothing to do with the gospel being preached. They formed another gospel, a social gospel that would exalt relationships and feelings above biblical teachings. Vance Havner once said, "If they had a social gospel in the days of the prodigal son, somebody would have given him a bed and a sandwich and he never would have gone home."[48] This is the compelling appeal at the core of every cult. The vast majority of people who go into cultic environments do so *because they make me feel loved, and they make me feel special*. Of course, the love of God is not void of emotions, but it is not to be led by them. When an emergent church culture is established within the house of God, it is not

---

47. John MacArthur, *The Master's Plan for the Church* (Chicago: Moody Press, 1991), 84.
48. Dennis J. Hester, *The Vance Havner Quote Book* (Grand Rapids: Baker Publishing Group, 1986).

THE UTOPIA OF A STRANGE LOVE

uncommon to hear that loving Jesus is greater than teaching about Him. *We don't need doctrine—it only divides. Just give us Jesus.* That sort of sentiment sounds good, but without basic doctrinal teachings one cannot be introduced to the Jesus of scripture. What they will find is another spirit.

It is common to hear people say those concerned for biblical doctrine and traditional Christian teaching lack true love and compassion. They point to the church at Ephesus in the second chapter of Revelation as an example of those who major in doctrine but who lack a love for God and others.

> To the angel of the church in Ephesus write: These are the words of him who holds the seven stars in his right hand and walks among the seven golden lampstands. I know your deeds, your hard work and your perseverance. I know that you cannot tolerate wicked people, that you have tested those who claim to be apostles but are not, and have found them false. You have persevered and have endured hardships for my name, and have not grown weary. Yet I hold this against you: You have forsaken the love you had at first. Consider how far you have fallen! Repent and do the things you did at first. If you do not repent, I will come to you and remove your lampstand from its place. But you have this in your favor: You hate the practices of the Nicolaitans, which I also hate. Whoever has ears, let them hear what the Spirit says to the churches. To the one who is victorious, I will give the right to eat from the tree of life, which is in the paradise of God. (Rev. 2:1-7)

The truth is that the church at Ephesus did not leave their first love because of doctrine but as a result of obligation. Their service to Christ had become mechanical; it had taken on an obligational tone. Therefore, they neglected the love they had for the Lord in the beginning. God frowns upon those who serve Him because they feel like they have to. He wants those who freely choose because they love. Freely choosing to serve God is the foundation of biblical love. Exercising biblical love is always a choice, never an obligation. It is choosing to love in spite of how one is treated. It is serving without receiving anything in return.

THE SECRET MEETING

True love is not sentimentalism. Showing true love is not about progress and working for humanity's self-improvement. Showing true love is not about being liked or admired. Showing true love is doing what is best for the other person in light of eternity. True love is telling sinners about their need for salvation. William Graham Scroggie once said, "It is possible to be led astray from the activity of true love by yielding to a false charity. At the very center of love is light. That is not true love, which sacrifices doctrine and principle. God has never acted in love at the expense of light."[49]

---

49. W. Graham Scroggie, *The Unfolding Drama of Redemption* (Grand Rapids: Kregal Classics, 1995).

THE LOVE OF GOD

A strange love has made its way into the church of God. It is a pseudo love that many embrace as if it is God's love. It is accepted like a child the night before Christmas, thinking a man in a red suit is delivering gifts while he sleeps. Because gifts do appear the next morning, the child is sure his feelings and beliefs are true. There is no telling him Santa does not exist; he has evidence and experience to the contrary.

This same sort of thing is happening in the church. Redefining the concept of God's love is misleading many. The apostle Paul told us "the time will come when people will not put up with sound doctrine. Instead, to suit their own desires, they will gather around them a great number of teachers to say what their itching ears want to hear. They will turn their ears away from the truth and turn aside to myths" (2 Tim. 4:3-4). The kind of myths he is speaking of are fables, fictitious narratives, falsehoods.

The Greek word for myths is *muthos*. Muthos is only used in a negative sense as something to be avoided, because it is false and unreal, fabricated by the mind in contrast to reality. Muthos refers to fictional viewpoints in contrast to true accounts, and it represents manufactured stories that have no basis in fact. I am afraid this is the strange version of love that many in the church today hold. The Old Testament tells when God gave Aaron, the high priest, instructions on how to offer up incense. God had a certain pattern every priest had to follow. But in the tenth chapter of Leviticus, it is recorded that Aaron's sons Nadab and Abihu offered incense to God and that God called the sacrifice "strange fire" or "unauthorized fire." The Hebrew meaning for this is profane, foreign, and counterfeit. God did not only reject this fire but it cost the two men their lives. "They offered unauthorized fire before the Lord, contrary to his command. So fire came out from the presence of the Lord and consumed them, and they died before the Lord. The Lord said, 'Among those who approach me I will be proved holy; in the sight of all the people I will be honored'" (Lev. 10:2-3). Aaron was struck with lament, but he remained silent.

Aaron's sons offered something that was not part of God's preordained order. They deviated from the Lord's instructions, and that was why their sacrifice was a counterfeit. Have we altered the love of God to something of our choosing? Have we confused the love of God with a strange love? How can we offer Him something pleasing when His doctrines have been forsaken? When we hear, "We don't need doctrine—it only divides. Just give us Jesus," are we giving God what we think He wants? Are we serving God based on His own will and desire, or ours? The root of all spiritual idolatry, from Adam and Eve in the Garden of Eden to the Last-Day church of the Laodiceans, is blatant insubordination. The enemy of our souls has convinced us that we can disregard what God has originally said without suffering any consequences for it.

What Is Biblical Love?

The love of God is not goosebump emotions. It is a truth that cannot be fully comprehended without consulting the full counsel of the scriptures. God's love intertwines with His attributes of justice, sovereignty, grace, peace, and wrath. When divine love is extracted to the exclusion of God's other attributes, it leads to a twisted view of what biblical love really is. Discovering the love of God apart from the full counsel of the Word of God is impossible. This is why Satan works overtime to remove sound teaching.

God's love is a very difficult concept. I have heard people express the opinion that God's love is simple, and one does not even need to know the Bible to understand it. I consider this nonsense. Others have said God's love is just about being obedient. Obedient to what? I suppose being obedient to one's feelings, performing good deeds, and living by human instincts. But none of this has to do with walking in the love of God. The Pharisees were proud of their works and their supposed obedience to God. Throughout the Gospels, they constantly rebuke Jesus concerning their misguided view of their relationship with the Father. In one such confrontation, Jesus responded with a scathing indictment when He told them, "I do not accept glory from human beings, but I know you. I know that you do not have the love of God in your hearts" (John 5:41-42). This verdict from Christ further escalated the contention between Himself and the Pharisees.

The Pharisees became convinced that Jesus was not sent from God, because surely, if anybody had love for God it would be them. After all, their works and "obedience" testified of their love. The only problem was that their works were based on the beliefs they formed for themselves, not what

THE LOVE OF GOD

the scriptures declared. Their extrabiblical interpretations canceled out the Word of God. According to Mark 7:13, "Thus you nullify the word of God by your tradition that you have handed down. And you do many things like that." It is a short step from fashioning our own system of thought to believing we are walking in God's love. Essentially, we become our own god! Satan will have his ministers always available to teach things confirming our own desires, bringing credibility to our error.

> In the presence of God and of Christ Jesus, who will judge the living and the dead, and in view of his appearing and his kingdom, I give you this charge: Preach the word; be prepared in season and out of season; correct, rebuke and encourage—with great patience and careful instruction. For the time will come when people will not put up with sound doctrine. Instead, to suit their own desires, they will gather around them a great number of teachers to say what their itching ears want to hear. They will turn their ears away from the truth and turn aside to myths. (2 Tim. 4:1-4)

Numerous verses of scripture talk about the love of God. One in particular goes to great lengths to explain God's love and the love of those who know Him:

> Dear friends, let us love one another, for love comes from God. Everyone who loves has been born of God and knows God. Whoever does not love does not know God, because God is love. This is how God showed his love among us: He sent his one and only Son into the world that we might live through him. This is love: not that we loved God, but that he loved us and sent his Son as an atoning sacrifice for our sins. Dear friends, since God so loved us, we also ought to love one another. (1 John 4:7-11)

This text from 1 John assures us that God is love, and those who serve Him must walk in that love. In addition, "Whoever does not love does not know God." The Greek word used for love in this verse is *agape*. Agape is a love that is produced by the will. It is a love that is fully devoted to an object. God's love is based on His choice, and it is rooted in His mercy. We see this

THE UTOPIA OF A STRANGE LOVE

fundamental principle in God's choice of Israel. God loved the nation of Israel because He chose to love her. He chose to love her because of a covenant He made with Abraham:

> The Lord did not set his affection on you and choose you because you were more numerous than other peoples, for you were the fewest of all peoples. But it was because the Lord loved you and kept the oath he swore to your ancestors that he brought you out with a mighty hand and redeemed you from the land of slavery, from the power of Pharaoh king of Egypt. (Deut. 7:7-8)

God's love is an amazing thing to behold. There was nothing in Israel or done by Israel to recommend God's favor. Yet God always keeps His word. He brought the Jews out of Egypt with a mighty hand because He swore an oath to Abraham. God was a debtor to His own promise, and He would fulfil that promise despite Israel's unworthiness.

Most people, whether religious or not, will say they believe God is loving. It is for this very reason Satan and his seducing spirits seek to hijack the concept of God's love. The tactic is to twist biblical dogmas so people can appear more loving to sinners. But God's love is always balanced with His wrath. The apostle Paul told us to "consider therefore the kindness and sternness of God: sternness to those who fell, but kindness to you, provided that you continue in his kindness. Otherwise, you also will be cut off" (Rom. 11:22). If we reject the notion of divine wrath, then our notion of divine love is not viewed through the lens of historic Christianity. It is not Bible based. Consider this: "Love must be sincere. Hate what is evil; cling to what is good" (Rom. 12:9). Love and hate are not rivals. A love that does not hate is not biblical love. A love that does not imply wrath is not scriptural.

The "New Cross"

In the emergent church's new age quest to become more culturally friendly, they have bought into an universalist view of love that hell and eternal punishment is not literal because of God's all-embracing acceptance. God's wrath is rejected as a carnal, juvenile, irrational response. This has happened because God has been reduced down to a mere human, while humanity has been deified. We see God and His actions through the lens of

THE LOVE OF GOD

human understanding and reasoning. Forgotten in the emerging thinkers' approach is that God's love is not like our love, nor is God's anger like our anger. In explaining God's wrath, John Stott says, "It does not mean . . . that he is likely to fly off the handle at the most trivial provocation, still less that he loses his temper for no apparent reason at all. For there is nothing capricious or arbitrary about the holy God. Nor is he ever irascible, malicious, spiteful or vindictive. His anger is neither mysterious nor irrational. It is never unpredictable but always predictable, because it is provoked by evil and by evil alone."[50]

Anthropomorphism is when we try describing God in terms of our own human understanding. The dictionary says it is "an interpretation of what is not human or personal in terms of human or personal characteristics." Throughout the Bible, phrases occur revealing examples of anthropomorphism. For example, we read verses where "God remembers," "the Lord changed his mind," and "the Lord regretted." Even though God allows Himself to be described in these terms, in order for us to understand what He is like, it is important we know that these descriptions are true by analogies and they are not unambiguous.

Anthropomorphic concepts apply not only to God's wrath but also in reference to God's love. Are we guilty of equating God's love with human love? Yes, and this has become the fuel on the fire of a strange love. J. I. Packer said, "God is not just—that is, he does not act in the way that is right, he does not do what is proper to a judge—unless he inflicts upon all sin and wrongdoing the penalty it deserves."[51] What makes God just and loving is that His wrath is justified. God's wrath and love are conjointly highlighted at the Cross. If we fail to view the Cross from a biblical point of view, we will eventually build our life around a Christianity that makes no unpleasant demands on us—what A. W. Tozer called "the new cross."[52] If you ask the

---

50. John Stott, *The Cross of Christ* (Leicester: Inter-Varsity Press, 1986), 173.
51. J. I. Packer, *Knowing God* (Leicester: Inter-Varsity Press, 1993), 207.
52. From "The Old Cross and the New," by A. W. Tozer. *The Alliance Witness*, July 24, 1963, Used with Permission. "All unannounced and mostly undetected. There has come in modern times a new cross into popular evangelical circles. It is like the old cross, but different: the likenesses are superficial; the differences, fundamental. From this new cross has sprung a new philosophy of the Christian life, and from that new philosophy has come a new evangelical technique—a new type of meeting and a new kind of preaching. This new evangelism employs the same language as the old, but its content is not the same and its emphasis not as before. The old cross would have no truck with the world. For Adam's

THE UTOPIA OF A STRANGE LOVE

proud flesh it meant the end of the journey. It carried into effect the sentence imposed by the law of Sinai. The new cross is not opposed to the human race; rather, it is a friendly pal and, if understood aright, it is the source of oceans of good clean fun and innocent enjoyment. It lets Adam live without interference. His life motivation is unchanged; he still lives for his own pleasure, only now he takes delight in singing choruses and watching religious movies instead of singing bawdy songs and drinking hard liquor. The accent is still on enjoyment, though the fun is now on a higher plane morally if not intellectually. The new cross encourages a new and entirely different evangelistic approach. The evangelist does not demand abnegation of the old life before a new life can be received. He preaches not contrasts but similarities. He seeks to key into public interest by showing that Christianity makes no unpleasant demands; rather, it offers the same thing the world does, only on a higher level. Whatever the sin-mad world happens to be clamoring after at the moment is cleverly shown to be the very thing the gospel offers, only the religious product is better. The new cross does not slay the sinner, it redirects him. It gears him into a cleaner and jollier way of living and saves his self-respect. To the self-assertive it says, 'Come and assert yourself for Christ.' To the egotist it says, 'Come and do your boasting in the Lord.' To the thrill seeker it says, 'Come and enjoy the thrill of Christian fellowship.' The Christian message is slanted in the direction of the current vogue in order to make it acceptable to the public. The philosophy back of this kind of thing may be sincere but its sincerity does not save it from being false. It is false because it is blind. It misses completely the whole meaning of the cross. The old cross is a symbol of death. It stands for the abrupt, violent end of a human being. The man in Roman times who took up his cross and started down the road had already said goodbye to his friends. He was not coming back. He was going out to have it ended. The cross made no compromise, modified nothing, spared nothing; it slew all of the man, completely and for good. It did not try to keep on good terms with its victim. It struck cruel and hard, and when it had finished its work, the man was no more. The race of Adam is under a death sentence. There is no commutation and no escape. God cannot approve any of the fruits of sin, however innocent they may appear or beautiful to the eyes of men. God salvages the individual by liquidating him and then raising him again to newness of life. That evangelism which draws friendly parallels between the ways of God and the ways of men is false to the Bible and cruel to the souls of its hearers. The faith of Christ does not parallel the world, it intersects it. In coming to Christ we do not bring our old life up onto a higher plane; we leave it at the cross. The corn of wheat must fall into the ground and die. We who preach the gospel must not think of ourselves as public relations agents sent to establish good will between Christ and the world. We must not imagine ourselves commissioned to make Christ acceptable to big business, the press, or the world of sports or modern education. We are not diplomats but prophets, and our message is not a compromise but an ultimatum. God offers life, but not an improved old life. The life He offers is life out of death. It stands always on the far side of the cross. Whoever would possess it must pass under the rod. He must repudiate himself and concur in God's just sentence against him. What does this mean to the individual, the condemned man who would find life in Christ Jesus? How can this theology be translated into life? Simply, he must repent and believe. He must forsake his sins and then go on to forsake himself. Let him cover nothing, defend nothing, excuse nothing. Let him not seek to make terms with

THE LOVE OF GOD

majority of people in today's church what word comes to mind concerning the Cross, the answer will be *love*. They are not wrong in this, but they are incomplete. An incomplete view leads to error. The Cross of Christ represents God's tremendous love for us, but it also represents God's wrath poured out on His only begotten Son. "For God so loved the world that he gave his one and only Son, that whoever believes in him shall not perish but have eternal life" (John 3:16). Yet this biblical truth is being swept away by the "new cross" of modern-day Marcionism.

The conflict between God's love and God's anger surfaced a few years ago over the song, "In Christ Alone." The hymn has become one of today's most popular worship songs. According to Christian Copyright Licensing International, "In Christ Alone" consistently ranks in the top songs sung in churches of all ethnicities and denominations. This song made headlines due to a Presbyterian Church U. S. A. hymn committee asking the songwriters for permission to print an altered version of one of the songs' original verses.[53] They wanted to change the line, "Till on the cross as Jesus died / the wrath of God was satisfied" to "Till on the cross as Jesus died / the love of God was magnified." The songwriters rejected the idea, and of course, the committee voted the song out. The chair of the committee thought the view that the cross is primarily about God's need to assuage His anger would have a negative effect on the hymnal's ability to form the faith of coming generations.

When this surfaced, it was found that years before another hymnal publisher had taken the liberty to change the same verse in "In Christ Alone" without permission from the copyright holder. Their hymnal was called *Celebrating Grace*. While the song writers were able to take a stand for biblical truth against the Presbyterian Church U. S. A. hymn committee, the

---

God, but let him bow his head before the stroke of God's stern displeasure and acknowledge himself worthy to die. Having done this let him gaze with simple trust upon the risen Savior, and from Him will come life and rebirth and cleansing and power. The cross that ended the earthly life of Jesus now puts an end to the sinner; and the power that raised Christ from the dead now raises him to a new life along with Christ. To any who may object to this or count it merely a narrow and private view of truth, let me say God has set His hallmark of approval upon this message from Paul's day to the present. Whether stated in these exact words or not, this has been the content of all preaching that has brought life and power to the world through the centuries."

53. The Gospel Coalition, Collin Hansen with Keith Getty, "What Makes 'In Christ Alone' Accepted and Contested," December 9, 2013.

THE UTOPIA OF A STRANGE LOVE

Celebrating Grace publishers never gave them the chance. We need more men and women who understand that our doxology must be supported by our theology. Warren Wierbe said, "For too many songs not only teach no doctrine, but many even teach false doctrines. A singer has no more right to sing a lie than a teacher has to teach a lie."[54] The wrath of God poured out on Christ is the essential doctrine of propitiation, which has to do with Jesus' atoning sacrifice for us as described in scripture. Paul stated in Romans that "God demonstrates his own love for us in this: While we were still sinners, Christ died for us. Since we have now been justified by his blood, how much more shall we be saved from God's wrath through him!" (5:8-9).

If we remove the idea of God's wrath being satisfied when Jesus died on the cross, we abandon the biblical cross for a new cross. Satan knows this and works to this end, for what would he like more than Christians worshiping an imaginary Jesus? We are living in such a day that we need to allow the Holy Spirit to strip us of all teaching we have embraced contrary to biblical truths. Without the proper biblical and theological foundation to weather the enormous error flooding our churches, we will never begin to understand God's true love.

---

54. Warren W. Wiersbe, *Be Faithful* (Colorado Springs: David C. Cook, 2009).

THE AGAPE DECEPTION

"God's love for me is agape, and it is unconditional." This phrase has been used so repeatedly among believers that to speak anything contrary is like signing one's own death warrant. Men whom we have admired throughout the ages have written books and preached sermons on the love of God from which have shaped and developed our views concerning this subject. What are some of the things that we have learned? From such men we have learned that there are four levels of love: *eros*, *storge*, *phileo*, and *agape*. Eros is love that extends from the heart, and it is romantic in type. Storge is the kind of love that is founded on family loyalty and duty. Phileo is brotherly love; it is humanity's love for one another and the lessor form of love when compared to agape. Lastly, there is agape love. We have been taught that this is the highest form of love—the type that only Christians can exhibit as it is selfless, divine, and unconditional. But is agape really unconditional? Is agape divine love? Is phileo the lessor love?

In this chapter, we will look at agape and phileo, due to the frequency of their use today. As stated, agape has been commonly taught as divine and unconditional love, while phileo is a lesser form of agape—brotherly love. How did the concept of unconditional love originate? Before we move forward, I believe it's important that we first define unconditional love. The dictionary says, "It is the acceptance of a person without them meeting any conditions. Affection that has no limitation. To cherish someone regardless of their character."[55] Is this what the Bible teaches? Clearly not. Does God extend His love toward all mankind without partiality? Yes. John 3:16 states that "for God so loved the world that he gave his one and only Son, that whoever believes in him shall not perish but have eternal life." But to define it as unconditional is misleading and eternally dangerous.

"Unconditional love" has never been a biblical concept. It was first coined by a German psychoanalyst named Erich Fromm in 1934. The idea was further developed in his successful 1956 book, *The Art of Loving*. Fromm rejected all forms of authoritarian government including God's. He viewed the God of the Old Testament as a self-seeking authoritarian. He was a

---

55. Wiktionary.com

THE UTOPIA OF A STRANGE LOVE

vowed atheist who vehemently argued against the teachings of the Christian faith. He believed that man is the measure of all things. He taught that a person must love himself, accept himself, and esteem himself in order to reach his highest potential. He believed that a father's love was always conditional—while a mother's was unconditional and couldn't be forfeited by sins or transgression. His ideas were later refined in the 1960s by a famous humanist psychologist named Carl Rogers.[56]

Rogers' parents were devout Protestants, and he enrolled in seminary school but later dropped out and abandoned Christianity for New Age mysticism. Rogers, skilled in the Greek language, defined agape as unconditional, but termed it "unconditional positive regard." It is the basic acceptance and support of a person regardless of what the person says or does. It is to always approve someone by setting aside your personal opinions and biases. It is the ability to isolate behaviors from the person who displays them. Does this sound familiar? How many times have you heard someone say, "God loves the sinner but hates the sin"? Is this biblical? Yes and no. If you are making reference to His love for the sinner in that He gave His Son for the sake of redemption, then yes. But if it's used to justify and accept wayward behavior without accountability, then no. You cannot separate sinners from their sins. What made them a sinner is their sin. God does not cast the sin into the lake of fire. He will cast the person who died in their sin into the fire.

This view of agape is contrary to apostolic teachings. It is humanistic psychology which is the workings of seducing spirits influencing the wisdom of men. Paul warned the church at Colossae concerning this issue: "And now, just as you accepted Christ Jesus as your Lord, you must continue to follow him. Let your roots grow down into him, and let your lives be built on him. Then your faith will grow strong in the truth you were taught, and you will overflow with thankfulness. Don't let anyone lead you away with empty philosophies and high-sounding nonsense that come from human thinking and from the spiritual powers of this world, rather than from Christ" (Col 2:6-8).

As stated previously, phileo is a type of love that has also been distorted in our time. It is said that phileo is shared mostly by the worldly and unregenerate. The words *agape* and *phileo* have become something like urban legends, anecdotes based on hearsay and widely circulated as true. In

---

56. Anne Karpf, "An Empty Kind of Love," December 2002.

the church, many things have been said about these terms that are untrue. Whereas phileo has been taught as brotherly love, it has also been taught that only those who are not Christians express it. In that way, it is a *lesser* form of love than agape. Yet some Bible texts teach otherwise:

> For the Father loves [phileo] the Son and shows him all he does. Yes, and he will show him even greater works than these, so that you will be amazed. (John 5:20)

> So the sisters sent word to Jesus, "Lord, the one you love [phileo] is sick." (John 11:3)

> Then the Jews said, "See how he loved [phileo] him!" (John 11:36)

> No, the Father himself loves [phileo] you because you have loved [phileo] me and have believed that I came from God. (John 16:27)

> So she came running to Simon Peter and the other disciple, the one Jesus loved [phileo], and said, "They have taken the Lord out of the tomb, and we don't know where they have put him!" (John 20:2)

> If anyone does not love [phileo] the Lord, let that person be cursed! (1 Cor. 16:22)

> Those whom I love [phileo] I rebuke and discipline. So be earnest and repent. (Rev. 3:19)

These scripture verses and others clearly show us we have been taught a distorted view of phileo. Yet even greater damage has been done to agape. We have been led to believe that agape is God's divine love. And because it is divine, we have been told it is unconditional and never ceases. First John 4 has been used to convince the masses that this is absolutely the meaning of agape.

THE UTOPIA OF A STRANGE LOVE

> Dear friends, let us love [agape] one another, for love [agape] comes from God. Everyone who loves [agape] has been born of God and knows God. Whoever does not love [agape] does not know God, because God is love [agape]. (1 John 4:7-8)

These verses use agape in reference to God five times. If this reference could be taken alone, we could indeed hold that agape means divine love. But what is missing is correlation. How does 1 John 4:7-8 correlate with other texts referencing agape? It is highly important for us to learn this principle. Imposters and deceivers will steadily increase as we approach the return of our Lord, and Peter left some weighty words on this in his second Epistle to the church:

> And so, dear friends, while you are waiting for these things to happen, make every effort to be found living peaceful lives that are pure and blameless in his sight. And remember, our Lord's patience gives people time to be saved. This is what our beloved brother Paul also wrote to you with the wisdom God gave him—speaking of these things in all of his letters. Some of his comments are hard to understand, and those who are ignorant and unstable have twisted his letters to mean something quite different, just as they do with other parts of Scripture. And this will result in their destruction. You already know these things, dear friends. So be on guard; then you will not be carried away by the errors of these wicked people and lose your own secure footing. Rather, you must grow in the grace and knowledge of our Lord and Savior Jesus Christ. All glory to him, both now and forever! Amen. (2 Pet. 3: 14-18 NLT)

Other verses besides 1 John 4:7-8 show us that agape can mean different things than divine love or unconditional love:

> Woe to you Pharisees, because you love [agape] the most important seats in the synagogues and respectful greetings in the marketplaces. (Luke 11:43)

No one can serve two masters. Either you will hate the one and love [agape] the other, or you will be devoted to the one and despise the other. You cannot serve both God and money. (Luke 16:13)

This is the verdict: Light has come into the world, but people loved [agape] darkness instead of light because their deeds were evil. (John 3:19)

. . . for they loved [agape] human praise more than praise from God. (John 12:43)

Demas, because he loved [agape] this world, has deserted me and has gone to Thessalonica. Crescens has gone to Galatia, and Titus to Dalmatia. (2 Tim. 4:10)

They have left the straight way and wandered off to follow the way of Balaam son of Bezer, who loved [agape] the wages of wickedness. (2 Pet. 2:15)

Do not love [agape] the world or anything in the world. If anyone loves the world, love for the Father is not in them. (1 John 2:15)

Paul Prophesied These Days Would Come

In the previous verses in which all of them use a form of agape, it is impossible to translate agape as divine love or love from God. Is it divine love that we love money or human praise? Is it the love of God that men desire darkness? Is it really God's love that we love the world—or seats in the synagogues? In 2 Samuel 13 there is the story about Amnon having love for his sister, Tamar. In the Septuagint, the translation of the Old Testament into Greek, the word used four times to describe Amnon's love for Tamar is translated agape. Verses 14-15 say, "But he refused to listen to her, and since he was stronger than she, he raped her. Then Amnon hated her with intense hatred. In fact, he hated her more than he had loved her. Amnon said to her, 'Get up and get out.'" If agape means God's love, or divine love, how could it lead to rape?

THE UTOPIA OF A STRANGE LOVE

If the scripture text does not fit, the teaching or doctrine is not legit! Do men love darkness unconditionally? Did Demas love the world in a divine way? Do people have a God kind of love for money? People love darkness, the world, human praise, and money because these things bring them something back in return. They certainly don't love them unconditionally.

Other scriptures show that agape is conditional:

If you love [agape] me, keep my commands. (John 14:15)

Whoever has my commands and keeps them is the one who loves [agape] me. The one who loves [agape] me will be loved [agape] by my Father, and I too will love [agape] them and show myself to them. (John 14:21)

Jesus replied, "Anyone who loves [agape] me will obey my teaching. My Father will love [agape] them, and we will come to them and make our home with them." (John 14:23)

Again, the point is that agape love is not unconditional. We will receive the agape love of Christ—*if* we keep His commands. The Father will agape love us—*if* we love Christ and obey His teaching. The life-giving promises of Jesus are always conditional:

Jesus straightened up and asked her, "Woman, where are they? Has no one condemned you?" "No one, sir," she said. "Then neither do I condemn you," Jesus declared. "Go now and leave your life of sin." (John 8:10-11)

Later Jesus found him at the temple and said to him, "See, you are well again. Stop sinning or something worse may happen to you." (John 5:14)

To the Jews who had believed him, Jesus said, "If you hold to my teaching, you are really my disciples. Then you will know the truth, and the truth will set you free." (John 8:31-32)

> You study the Scriptures diligently because you think that in them you have eternal life. These are the very Scriptures that testify about me, yet you refuse to come to me to have life. (John 5:39-40)

> Whoever believes in him is not condemned, but whoever does not believe stands condemned already because they have not believed in the name of God's one and only Son. (John 3:18)

We can use the same vocabulary, but if our vocabulary has the wrong definition, we will worship another Jesus. Paul warned that "if someone comes to you and preaches a Jesus other than the Jesus we preached, or if you receive a different spirit from the Spirit you received, or a different gospel from the one you accepted, you put up with it easily enough" (2 Cor. 11:4). J.C Ryle (1816–1900), the first Anglican bishop of Liverpool, wrote, "There is a quantity of half-truth taught by the modern false teachers: they are incessantly using Scriptural terms and phrases in an unscriptural sense."[57]

---

57. J. C. Ryle (1816–1900), *Warnings to the Churches* (Scotland: Banner of Truth Trust, 1967), 77-79, Used with Permission. In this book, Ryle addresses the many dangers facing the church in his time and dangers that are still plaguing the church today. In discussing the perils of chasing after "diverse and strange doctrines" (Heb. 13:9), he placed an emphasis for Christians to go back and be avid students and readers of the scriptures. In his passionate plea as a true pastor and watchman, Ryle said, "Many things combine to make the present inroad of false doctrine peculiarly dangerous. There is an undeniable zeal in some of the teachers of error: their 'earnestness' (to use an unhappy cant phrase) makes many think they must be right. There is a great appearance of learning and theological knowledge; many fancy that such clever and intellectual men must surely be safe guides. There is a general tendency to free thought and free inquiry in these latter days; many like to prove their independence of judgment by believing novelties. There is a widespread desire to appear charitable and liberal-minded; many seem half ashamed of saying that anybody can be in the wrong. There is a quantity of half-truth taught by the modern false teachers; they are incessantly using scriptural terms and phrases in an unscriptural sense. There is a morbid craving in the public mind for a more sensuous, ceremonial, sensational, showy worship: men are impatient of inward, invisible heart-work. There is a silly readiness in every direction to believe everybody who talks cleverly, lovingly, and earnestly, and a determination to forget that Satan is often 'transformed into an angel of light' (2 Cor. 11:14). There is a widespread 'gullibility' among professing Christians; every heretic who tells his story plausibly is sure to be believed, and everybody who doubts him is called a persecutor and a narrow-minded man. All these things are peculiar symptoms of our times. I defy any

THE UTOPIA OF A STRANGE LOVE

Why does Satan work to convince the church that God's love is unconditional? It is in order to promote lives of disobedience, to remove the fear of God, and to strip away the belief of God's wrath. The enemy ultimately desires us to nullify Jesus' death on the cross. If I am convinced God's love is unconditional, I can pick and choose what scripture to obey. There is no reason why I should repent and be converted. I can live my life to please myself, and I can live without conviction. Why would God require a Lord-and-slave relationship?

Several years ago, I was teaching a series entitled, "The Eternity-Driven Life." The messages were about the cost and the requirements of true Christian discipleship, and they were based on the ninth chapter of the Gospel of Luke, including, "Whoever wants to be my disciple must deny themselves and take up their cross daily and follow me. For whoever wants to save their life will lose it, but whoever loses their life for me will save it. What good is it for someone to gain the whole world, and yet lose or forfeit their very self?" (Luke 9:23-25). When the service was over, a guest told a member of our church, "This doesn't apply to us today, so I don't know what he is talking about. My God is not like that." How could anyone think the command to deny ourselves was out of date? Upon inquiry, this person attended a church that heavily emphasized God's unconditional love. We are living in a day when teaching that confronts self-centered living will be scorned and ridiculed.

---

observing man to deny them. They tend to make the assaults of false doctrine in our day peculiarly dangerous. They make it more than ever needful to cry aloud, 'Be not carried about.' Does anyone ask me, 'What is the best safeguard against false doctrine?' I answer in one word, 'The Bible: the Bible regularly read, regularly prayed over, regularly studied.' We must go back to the old prescription of our Master: 'Search the Scriptures' (John 5:39). If we want a weapon to wield against the devices of Satan, there is nothing like 'the sword of the Spirit, the Word of God.' But to wield it successfully, we must read it habitually, diligently, intelligently, and prayerfully. This is a point on which, I fear, many fail. In an age of hurry and bustle, few read their Bibles as much as they should. More books perhaps are read than ever, but less of the one Book which makes man wise unto salvation. Rome and neology could never have made such havoc in the church in the last fifty years if there had not been a most superficial knowledge of the scriptures throughout the land. A Bible-reading laity is the strength of a church." If we would not be carried about by "diverse and strange doctrines," we must remember the words of our Lord Jesus Christ: "Search the Scriptures." Ignorance of the Bible is the root of all error. Knowledge of the Bible is the best antidote against modern heresies.

THE AGAPE DECEPTION

This individual's reaction is but a picture of what is happening in the body of Christ at large. Any teaching critical of self being glorified is labeled unloving and negative. These are the days the apostle Paul prophesied would come. Before Paul's time was up here on earth, he said,

> For the time will come when people will not put up with sound doctrine. Instead, to suit their own desires, they will gather around them a great number of teachers to say what their itching ears want to hear. They will turn their ears away from the truth and turn aside to myths. (2 Tim. 4:3-4)

The scriptures point out very clearly the grave danger of living for and loving self. A church culture consisting of lovers of self is the first sign of perilous times, as Paul also told us: "Mark this: There will be terrible times in the last days" (2 Tim. 3:1).

A trip to a local bookstore will reveal such titles as, *Your Best Life Now; Love Your Life; It's Your Time: Activate Your Faith, Achieve Your Dreams, and Increase in God's Favor; Become A Better You; How to Succeed at being Yourself; God Wants You Happy; 8 Steps to Create the Life You Want; Instinct: The Power to Unleash Your Inborn Drive; You're All That; Love the Life You Live; The Power Of I Am;* and *Repositioning Yourself: Living Life without Limits.* One could expect seeing a list of such self-serving books at secular stores—perhaps under the New Age section—but this trip was to a Christian bookstore! These books are by well-known authors, though the actual writers may or may not be identified, who have accumulated a large following. Some of these books made the best-seller list. How can the Spirit of God inspire someone to write things contrary to scripture?

The answer is He cannot inspire someone to write things that twist the Bible's clear meaning. Why would followers of Jesus support such books that oppose the Lord's teachings? I believe a seducing spirit is at work telling us that God's love is unfailing and unconditional and that God wants us to live for and love ourselves. This behavior encourages a life of disobedience to the lordship of Christ over our lives and places us on a broad pathway to destruction. Instead, we are told to "enter through the narrow gate. For wide is the gate and broad is the road that leads to destruction, and many enter through it. But small is the gate and narrow the road that leads to life, and only a few find it" (Matt. 7:13-14).

THE UTOPIA OF A STRANGE LOVE

No Wrath, No Consequences

It is not convicting to walk on the broad pathway because, if God's love is unconditional, there is no wrath. If there is no wrath, there are no consequences. How can there be fear of God's wrath when questionable teachers have stripped the concept away? Satan's goal is to convince the church that hell could never be our destination, simply because we have confessed verbally that Jesus is our Savior. "For such people are false apostles, deceitful workers, masquerading as apostles of Christ. And no wonder, for Satan himself masquerades as an angel of light. It is not surprising, then, if his servants also masquerade as servants of righteousness. Their end will be what their actions deserve" (2 Cor. 11:13-15).

Satan and his deceitful workers use propaganda to condemn countless souls—not all come from the world, for many come from the church. The Bible teaches that hell and the lake of fire is the destination of those who reject Christ and His Word. Our decisions can make us friends or enemies with God, but ultimately, God's sovereignty and power will determine our outcomes. Jesus said, "I tell you, my friends, do not be afraid of those who kill the body and after that can do no more. But I will show you whom you should fear: Fear him who, after your body has been killed, has authority to throw you into hell. Yes, I tell you, fear him" (Luke 12:4-5).

Paul supports the righteous but warns false apostles who have not obeyed the gospel:

> God is just: He will pay back trouble to those who trouble you and give relief to you who are troubled, and to us as well. This will happen when the Lord Jesus is revealed from heaven in blazing fire with his powerful angels. He will punish those who do not know God and do not obey the gospel of our Lord Jesus. They will be punished with everlasting destruction and shut out from the presence of the Lord and from the glory of his might. (2 Thess. 1:6-9)

God's authoritative power can and will deliver men and women to hell. Does He do this while yet loving them? Clearly, no. An unbiblical view of God's love supplants belief in the wrath of God, but if there is no divine wrath, what did Christ's death and resurrection spare us from? "But God demonstrates his own love for us in this: While we were still sinners, Christ died for us. Since we have now been justified by his blood, how much more shall we be saved from God's wrath through him! For if, while we were God's enemies, we were reconciled to him through the death of his Son, how much more, having been reconciled, shall we be saved through his life!" (Rom. 5:8-10). Christ redeemed us from sin, because sin made us enemies with God, and therefore His wrath was upon us.

God's love is truly amazing. It is both phileo and agape, and it is beyond human comprehension. To know God's love is to know Him. His love compels us to no longer live life for ourselves but willingly to become His slaves, as the apostle Paul wrote: "For Christ's love compels us, because we are convinced that one died for all, and therefore all died. And he died for all, that those who live should no longer live for themselves but for him who died for them and was raised again" (2 Cor. 5:14-15). No one deserves God's love; therefore, we need to examine ourselves carefully to make sure we are not irreverent of His love.

To summarize, *phileo* means to cherish, to be fond of, to take strong delight in, or to like well. The word is associated with intense endearment, although brotherly love and unregenerate love is a stretch. Paul's closing remarks to the Christians in Corinth should make us rethink the idea that phileo is a lesser love: "If anyone does not love the Lord, let that person be cursed!" (1 Cor. 16:22). *Agape*, on the other hand, means to esteem, to honor, to value, or to respect. Agape represents devoted love for someone or something. Agape love is an act of the will, not the emotions, and it should not be defined as "divine love" or the "God kind of love." According to the scriptures, agape is not always unconditional. God functions in both phileo and agape types of love.

It is vital we divorce ourselves from erroneous teachings concerning God's love.

THE WRATH OF GOD

Some might say that God does not hate. If that is true, then God also does not love. The love and the wrath of God are not enemies or rivals trying to outdo one another. They are one, and they cannot be separated. As I stated in the last chapter, an unbiblical view of God's love supplants belief in the wrath of God, but if there is no divine wrath, what did Christ's death and resurrection spare us from? I will go further and say that if one does not know the wrath of God, it is impossible to know His love. The converse of this is also true: without knowing the love of God, there is no understanding His wrath.

What is the wrath of God? Let us begin by seeing what it is not. God's wrath has nothing to do with His being irritable, throwing a temper tantrum, or displaying uncontrollable anger. He is the God who vindicates, but His wrath is never vindictive. God's wrath is not malicious retaliation from the hand of the All-Powerful.

Rather, God's wrath is His settled hostility against sin and those who practice sin. It is a divine attribute of holiness moved into action against all unrighteousness. It is God's eternal displeasure directed to those who rebel against His authority and offend His sovereignty. The wrath of God is the justifiable indignation provoked by unsurrendered pride—His just, perfect, necessary, and righteous retribution against prolonged rejection of His lordship. His wrath is not an abstract quality, for it is part of His divine attributes just as much as love, goodness, grace, and mercy. If God is a God of love, He is also a God of wrath.

In an attempt to "win the world at any cost" (an unbiblical phrase), the modern church has suppressed historical biblical truths for the sake of not offending the sensitivities of the secular mindset. Many church leaders have taken the tack of the movie *Field of Dreams*—if we build it, they will come. Many local churches appeal almost exclusively to "seekers" rather than serious believers, and when this happens, they tend to be more consumer driven than God centered. These leaders have altered the mission of the church to appeal to dishonest seekers. God is presented as an "On Demand" genie that's too loving to make any demands. This is what happens when Madison Avenue advertising methods override the leading of the Holy

THE UTOPIA OF A STRANGE LOVE

Spirit. Yet this is nothing new. In Jesus' day, many were drawn to Him because of His miracles rather than His teaching. During one particular occasion, the feeding of the multitude, the people intended to seize Jesus to make Him king. For the sake of the miracle, nevertheless, He withdrew from this sort of attention:

> Jesus said, "Have the people sit down." There was plenty of grass in that place, and they sat down (about five thousand men were there). Jesus then took the loaves, gave thanks, and distributed to those who were seated as much as they wanted. He did the same with the fish. When they had all had enough to eat, he said to his disciples, "Gather the pieces that are left over. Let nothing be wasted." So they gathered them and filled twelve baskets with the pieces of the five barley loaves left over by those who had eaten. After the people saw the sign Jesus performed, they began to say, "Surely this is the Prophet who is to come into the world." Jesus, knowing that they intended to come and make him king by force, withdrew again to a mountain by himself. (John 6:10-15)

Jesus later rebuked the crowd for their superficial motives in pursuing Him. He never allowed the demands of the people to overrule the requirements of His Father. So far as He was concerned, there was no loophole in the Father's plan to meet the expectations of seekers.

What happens when seekers are placed in the hands of a worldly church? They are convinced they know God, and they are ready to meet Christ. They believe they are redeemed, but no true regeneration has taken place. They believe they are saved from the wrath of God, yet no sanctification has happened. They believe they are forgiven of their sins, but they have neglected repentance. In an effort to please these seekers, many churches have disregarded the wrath of God. I have even heard attempts to apologize for the concept of God's wrath itself, as though it is some shortcoming in God's character. In his book *The Attributes of God*, A. W. Pink said,

> It is sad to find so many professing Christians who appear to regard the wrath of God as something for which they need to make an apology, or at least they wish there were no such thing. While some would not go so far as to openly admit

that they consider it a blemish on the Divine character, yet they are far from regarding it with delight; they like not to think about it, and they rarely hear it mentioned without a secret resentment rising up in their hearts against it. Even with those who are more sober in their judgment, not a few seem to imagine that there is a severity about the Divine wrath, which is too terrifying to form a theme for profitable contemplation. Others harbor the delusion that God's wrath is not consistent with His goodness, and so seek to banish it from their thoughts. Yes, many there are who turn away from a vision of God's wrath as though they were called to look upon some blotch in the Divine character, or some blot upon the Divine government. But what saith the Scriptures? As we turn to them we find that God has made no attempt to conceal the fact of His wrath. He is not ashamed to make it known that vengeance and fury belong unto Him.[58]

We cannot hide from God's wrath, and we can never be ashamed of it. From Genesis to Revelation we witness the wrath of God revealed against the disobedience of humankind. Contrary to the current neo-Marcion movement, the God of the Old Testament is the same God of the New Testament. The Father proclaims, "I the Lord do not change" (Mal. 3:6). The Jews misdiagnosed God's justice and judgment. They developed a perception of God based on their own viewpoint that there was no difference between good and evil. They said, "All who do evil are good in the eyes of the Lord, and he is pleased with them" (Mal. 2:17). God responded by telling them the principles of right and wrong never change, just as He never changes. God's divine attributes will never change!

Sin in the World

I once heard a well-known pastor say that God only showed His anger because of the law and that divine wrath is never exhibited under grace. I was surprised to hear this from the pastor, because that statement alone indicated how much he misunderstood the Bible. God's wrath is provoked in the first eight chapter of Genesis—from the beginning of Creation to

---

58. A. W. Pink, *The Attributes of God* (Grand Rapids: Baker Books, 2006), chapter 16.

THE UTOPIA OF A STRANGE LOVE

Noah and the Flood—and this was before the giving of the law! God's wrath is revealed in the Garden of Eden against humankind because the first human pair disobeyed God's command that "you must not eat from the tree of the knowledge of good and evil, for when you eat from it you will certainly die" (Gen. 2:17). The result of this disobedience was that sin became a part of the human race:

> Now the serpent was more crafty than any of the wild animals the Lord God had made. He said to the woman, "Did God really say, 'You must not eat from any tree in the garden'?" The woman said to the serpent, "We may eat fruit from the trees in the garden, but God did say, 'You must not eat fruit from the tree that is in the middle of the garden, and you must not touch it, or you will die.'" "You will not certainly die," the serpent said to the woman. "For God knows that when you eat from it your eyes will be opened, and you will be like God, knowing good and evil." When the woman saw that the fruit of the tree was good for food and pleasing to the eye, and also desirable for gaining wisdom, she took some and ate it. She also gave some to her husband, who was with her, and he ate it. . . . To the woman [God] said, "I will make your pains in childbearing very severe; with painful labor you will give birth to children. Your desire will be for your husband, and he will rule over you." To Adam he said, "Because you listened to your wife and ate fruit from the tree about which I commanded you, 'You must not eat from it,' cursed is the ground because of you; through painful toil you will eat food from it all the days of your life." . . . So the Lord God banished [Adam and Eve] from the Garden of Eden to work the ground from which he had been taken. After he drove the man out, he placed on the east side of the Garden of Eden cherubim and a flaming sword flashing back and forth to guard the way to the tree of life. (Gen. 3:1-24)

Satan, in the form of the serpent, knew from experience that God's holiness would not tolerate rebellion. The consequence of rebellion was death and the removal of Adam and Eve (and their descendants) from God's presence.

THE WRATH OF GOD

God's wrath comes against Cain for the murder of his brother, Abel, in the early chapters of Genesis. "Now you are under a curse and driven from the ground, which opened its mouth to receive your brother's blood from your hand. When you work the ground, it will no longer yield its crops for you. You will be a restless wanderer on the earth." Cain said to the Lord, "My punishment is more than I can bear. Today you are driving me from the land, and I will be hidden from your presence" (Gen. 4:11-14).

The wrath of God is also displayed in the Flood during the times of Noah:

> When human beings began to increase in number on the earth and daughters were born to them, the sons of God saw that the daughters of humans were beautiful, and they married any of them they chose. Then the Lord said, "My Spirit will not contend with humans forever, for they are mortal; their days will be a hundred and twenty years." . . . The Lord said, "I will wipe from the face of the earth the human race I have created—and with them the animals, the birds and the creatures that move along the ground—for I regret that I have made them." But Noah found favor in the eyes of the Lord. . . . God saw how corrupt the earth had become, for all the people on earth had corrupted their ways. So God said to Noah, "I am going to put an end to all people, for the earth is filled with violence because of them. I am surely going to destroy both them and the earth. (Gen. 6:1-4, 7-8, 12-13)

God was very specific about the amount of time left to His creation to repent of their persistent evil: a hundred and twenty years. Still, men and women rejected God, causing the great Flood to engulf the earth and wipe out the entire human race, except for Noah and his family.

God's wrath is also revealed against the depravity of Sodom and Gomorrah, cities on the Jordan River plain in the land of Canaan. When their crimes against humanity reached a point of no return, God sent burning sulfur to consume the cities completely:

> Then the Lord said, "The outcry against Sodom and Gomorrah is so great and their sin so grievous that I will go

down and see if what they have done is as bad as the outcry that has reached me. If not, I will know." . . . Then the Lord rained down burning sulfur on Sodom and Gomorrah—from the Lord out of the heavens. Thus he overthrew those cities and the entire plain, destroying all those living in the cities—and also the vegetation in the land. (Gen. 18:20-21; 19:24-25)

In a similar way, we learn in the book of Jude, "Sodom and Gomorrah and the surrounding towns gave themselves up to sexual immorality and perversion. They serve as an example of those who suffer the punishment of eternal fire" (Jude 7). Their example instructs those who practice the same sin that their immorality and sexual perversion will bring the same eternal vengeance.

Another place exhibiting God's vengeance was the deliverance of the children of Israel out of Egypt. The plagues brought against Pharaoh in the seventh chapter of Exodus, and the perishing of the Egyptians in the Red Sea in the fourteenth chapter, was God's wrath in action against the Egyptians' false gods. Remember, all these events took place before the giving of the law. In his book *The Apostolic Preaching of the Cross*, Leon Morris says there are twenty words connected to the wrath of God in the Hebrew Bible, and these words are used more than five hundred eighty times.[59] J. A. Baird said, "Wherever in the Old Testament one finds a reference to the love of God, his wrath is always in the background, either explicitly or implicitly, and we neglect this element to the impoverishment of the Hebrew concept of love."[60] What about the New Testament?

God's Retribution in the New Testament

Like the pastor I mentioned earlier, many say God's wrath is found only in the Old Covenant. Because Jesus sacrificed Himself for us, we are no longer subject to God's retribution. I have heard people proclaim with great boldness, "We are under a better covenant, so we are never threatened by God's wrath." These people object to preachers talking about the wrath of God because, they claim, the New Testament never even uses the word

---

59. Leon Morris, *The Apostolic Preaching of the Cross* (Grand Rapids: Eerdmans, 1955), 131.
60. J. A. Baird, *The Justice of God in the Teaching of Jesus* (London: S.C.M., 1963), 46.

THE WRATH OF GOD

wrath. Well they are incorrect! The word is not only used in the New Testament but the concept of wrath is frequently presented—wrapped in such terms as *judgment, condemnation, hell,* and *destruction*. In fact, Jesus spoke more about hell than heaven. He spoke about God's wrath more than God's love. The teaching of the apostles is replete with the wrath-of-God terminology. J. C. Ryle wrote,

> Men have arisen in these latter days, who profess to deny the eternity of future punishment, and repeat the devil's old argument, that we "shall not surely die." Let none of their reasoning move us, however plausible they may sound. Let us stand fast in the old paths. The God of love and mercy is also a God of justice. He will surely requite. The flood in Noah's day, and the burning of Sodom, were meant to show us what He will one day do. No lips have ever spoken so clearly about hell as those of Christ Himself. Hardened sinners will find out, to their costs, that there is such a thing as the "wrath of the Lamb."[61]

If Christ, who is our Lord and Master, and who was led by the Spirit of God, spoke on the subjects of wrath, destruction, and hell more than God's love, who or what leads our leaders today?

The first voice in the New Testament that shakes the conscience of sin is John the Baptist, the forerunner of the promised Messiah. The prophet Isaiah foretold John's coming: "A voice of one calling: 'In the wilderness prepare the way for the Lord; make straight in the desert a highway for our God. Every valley shall be raised up, every mountain and hill made low; the rough ground shall become level, the rugged places a plain. And the glory of the Lord will be revealed, and all people will see it together. For the mouth of the Lord has spoken'" (Isa. 40:3-5). John's coming represents the mercy and the compassion of God, and His name actually means "Jehovah has shown grace." He was sent to prepare hearts for the coming of the Lamb. One of the first things John said to the crowds wanting to be baptized by him was, "You brood of vipers! Who warned you to flee from the coming wrath?" (Luke 3:7). After four hundred years of silence, John used the same vocabulary as the prophets of old.

---

61. J. C. Ryle, *Expository Thoughts on Matthew* (Scotland: Banner of Truth, 1986), 222.

THE UTOPIA OF A STRANGE LOVE

A common thread throughout the Word of God is that when the grace of God or the love of God appears, with it there will also be the wrath of God. These attributes are conjoined, and there is absolutely no incompatibility between them. Many try discrediting John's teaching on wrath by suggesting he represents only the Old Testament prophets. But when John asked, "Who warned you to flee from the coming wrath?" he was asking, "Who told you that you could escape from the punishment God is about to send?" John's message was not past tense; he was speaking of approaching wrath. In the Gospel of Matthew, written to the Jews, note the context of John's message:

> People went out to him from Jerusalem and all Judea and the whole region of the Jordan. Confessing their sins, they were baptized by him in the Jordan River. But when he saw many of the Pharisees and Sadducees coming to where he was baptizing, he said to them: "You brood of vipers! Who warned you to flee from the coming wrath? Produce fruit in keeping with repentance. And do not think you can say to yourselves, 'We have Abraham as our father.' I tell you that out of these stones God can raise up children for Abraham. The ax is already at the root of the trees, and every tree that does not produce good fruit will be cut down and thrown into the fire. I baptize you with water for repentance. But after me comes one who is more powerful than I, whose sandals I am not worthy to carry. He will baptize you with the Holy Spirit and fire. His winnowing fork is in his hand, and he will clear his threshing floor, gathering his wheat into the barn and burning up the chaff with unquenchable fire." (Matt. 3:5-12)

The thought of a Jew being a recipient of divine wrath was offensive, to say the least. John's sharp rebuke was the kind reserved for Gentiles. The ax of God's judgment and the burning up of the chaff with unquenchable fire speaks of God's final retribution. John the Baptist's message sets up a common theme that Jesus Himself follows, for when the Lord begins His ministry, His first public act is to demonstrate the wrath of God. He enters Jerusalem, makes a whip of cords, and drives the cattle, sheep, and dove sellers out of the temple.

THE WRATH OF GOD

> When it was almost time for the Jewish Passover, Jesus went up to Jerusalem. In the temple courts he found people selling cattle, sheep and doves, and others sitting at tables exchanging money. So he made a whip out of cords, and drove all from the temple courts, both sheep and cattle; he scattered the coins of the money changers and overturned their tables. To those who sold doves he said, "Get these out of here! Stop turning my Father's house into a market!" His disciples remembered that it is written: "Zeal for your house will consume me." (John 2:13-17)

John recorded the clearing of the temple at the beginning of his Gospel, whereas the synoptic Gospels record this scene at the end of Jesus' ministry. Most biblical students see that Jesus cleaned the temple twice. Instead of God's house being a place of prayer, it was turned into a safe haven for commercialization and extortion. The holiness of God demanded a necessary corrective action from Christ, thereby providing a picture of God's wrath.

Judgment Is at the Door

Countless churches today are magnets for modern-day moneychangers. Judgment is at the door, and repentance is required. When Jesus began His public ministry, He preached, "Repent, for the kingdom of heaven has come near" (Matt. 4:17). Jesus was a repentance preacher! Repentance was a constant theme in all His public teachings. When He was informed that Pilate butchered Jews from Galilee as they sacrificed at the temple in Jerusalem, Jesus preached repentance:

> Now there were some present at that time who told Jesus about the Galileans whose blood Pilate had mixed with their sacrifices. Jesus answered, "Do you think that these Galileans were worse sinners than all the other Galileans because they suffered this way? I tell you, no! But unless you repent, you too will all perish. Or those eighteen who died when the tower in Siloam fell on them—do you think they were more guilty than all the others living in Jerusalem? I tell you, no! But unless you repent, you too will all perish." (Luke 13:1-5)

THE UTOPIA OF A STRANGE LOVE

Some people say repentance (*metanoeo* in the Greek) just means to change one's mind. But it means more than that. Metanoeo suggests a radical turning away from a behavior or a sin. It is more than an intellectual idea. It stresses a person's turning around in his or her totality. Judas, for example, had a change of mind, which was brought on by remorse, but he did not have a change of heart. A change of heart is accompanied by repentance. "When Judas, who had betrayed him, saw that Jesus was condemned, he was seized with remorse and returned the thirty pieces of silver to the chief priests and the elders. 'I have sinned,' he said, 'for I have betrayed innocent blood'" (Matt. 27:3-4). True repentance would have turned Judas from his sin to plead to God for mercy. Instead, he looked for an opportunity to self-medicate his guilt, which in his case led to suicide. "So Judas threw the money into the temple and left. Then he went away and hanged himself" (Matt. 27:5).

Louis Berkhof describes biblical repentance as a change of view, a change of feeling, and a change of purpose. He writes that it is "a change of view, a recognition of sin as involving personal guilt, defilement, and helplessness; a change of feeling, manifesting itself in sorrow for sin committed against a holy God; a change of purpose, an inward turning away from sin, and a disposition to seek pardon and cleansing."[62] This view of penitence is severely absent in the life of the church today. Simply "asking God to forgive us" is less offensive to seeker friendly audiences than recognizing our dire situation of guilt and defilement and our need of pardon and cleansing. But if it does not lead to eternal fruit, "asking God to forgive us" is futile.

Jesus mentioned the sign of Jonah and the men of Nineveh in the Gospel of Luke. What did Jonah preach, and what was the response of the people of Nineveh?

> Jonah began by going a day's journey into the city, proclaiming, "Forty more days and Nineveh will be overthrown." The Ninevites believed God. A fast was proclaimed, and all of them, from the greatest to the least, put on sackcloth. When Jonah's warning reached the king of Nineveh, he rose from his throne, took off his royal robes, covered himself with sackcloth and sat down in the dust.

---

62. Louis Berkhof, *Systematic Theology* (Grand Rapids: Eerdmans, 1939), 492.

This is the proclamation he issued in Nineveh: "By the decree of the king and his nobles: Do not let people or animals, herds or flocks, taste anything; do not let them eat or drink. But let people and animals be covered with sackcloth. Let everyone call urgently on God. Let them give up their evil ways and their violence. Who knows? God may yet relent and with compassion turn from his fierce anger so that we will not perish." When God saw what they did and how they turned from their evil ways, he relented and did not bring on them the destruction he had threatened. (Jon. 3:4-10)

Once again we see the grace and mercy of God in the Old Testament. Jesus preached repentance because He knew judgment awaited those rejecting His offer of salvation.

THE SERMON ON THE MOUNT

The Sermon on the Mount is one of the so-called five discourses in the Gospel of Matthew. It is the longest teaching of Jesus in the New Testament, and it takes place early in His ministry. The sermon begins in the fifth chapter of Matthew and runs throughout chapter seven. It is Christ's skillful exposition of the law and His rebuke and correction of the Pharisaic interpretation of the law. The Sermon on the Mount should be the foundation and hallmark of every believer's Christian walk.

In part of the sermon, Jesus speaks of God's wrath by referencing hell and eternal punishment:

> I tell you that anyone who is angry with a brother or sister be subject to judgment. Again, anyone who says to a brother or sister, "Raca," is answerable to the court. And anyone who says, "You fool!" will be in danger of the fire of hell. . . . If your right eye causes you to stumble, gouge it out and throw it away. It is better for you to lose one part of your body than for your whole body to be thrown into hell. And if your right hand causes you to stumble, cut it off and throw it away. It is better for you to lose one part of your body than for your whole body to go into hell. (Matt. 5:22, 29-30)

Jesus also speaks of destruction: "Enter through the narrow gate. For wide is the gate and broad is the road that leads to destruction, and many enter through it" (Matt. 7:13). Reference to eternal fire is also found in the sermon: "Every tree that does not bear good fruit is cut down and thrown into the fire" (Matt. 7:19). Jesus concludes his sermon with talk of eternal devastation: "The rain came down, the streams rose, and the winds blew and beat against that house, and it fell with a great crash" (Matt. 7:27).

All of this is to say that Jesus spoke more about hell, eternal punishment, and destruction of the soul than any other theme. When one

THE UTOPIA OF A STRANGE LOVE

peruses the Gospel of Matthew alone, the theme of God's wrath occurs repeatedly. In Matthew 10:11-15, Jesus instructs the disciples that those who gladly receive the gospel are happy, but those who refuse it will stand in judgment:

> Whatever town or village you enter, search there for some worthy person and stay at their house until you leave. As you enter the home, give it your greeting. If the home is deserving, let your peace rest on it; if it is not, let your peace return to you. If anyone will not welcome you or listen to your words, leave that home or town and shake the dust off your feet. Truly I tell you, it will be more bearable for Sodom and Gomorrah on the day of judgment than for that town.

The command to "shake the dust off your feet" in this text has a symbolic threefold meaning. First, it was common for Jews to shake the dust off their feet when returning from Gentile towns. Doing so was an expression of contempt, for it labeled that town as pagan in the eyes of God. Second, the phrase also testifies that the apostles had done their jobs and had washed their hands of any future responsibility. The apostle Paul had this concept in mind when he said, "I declare to you today that I am innocent of the blood of any of you" in Acts 20:26. In other words, "My hands are clean. It is not my fault." The idea was derived from God's charge to Ezekiel as His watchman:

> The word of the Lord came to me: "Son of man, speak to your people and say to them: 'When I bring the sword against a land, and the people of the land choose one of their men and make him their watchman, and he sees the sword coming against the land and blows the trumpet to warn the people, then if anyone hears the trumpet but does not heed the warning and the sword comes and takes their life, their blood will be on their own head. Since they heard the sound of the trumpet but did not heed the warning, their blood will be on their own head. If they had heeded the warning, they would have saved themselves. But if the watchman sees the sword coming and does not blow the trumpet to warn the people and the sword comes and takes someone's life, that person's

THE SERMON ON THE MOUNT

> life will be taken because of their sin, but I will hold the watchman accountable for their blood.' Son of man, I have made you a watchman for the people of Israel; so hear the word I speak and give them warning from me. When I say to the wicked, 'You wicked person, you will surely die,' and you do not speak out to dissuade them from their ways, that wicked person will die for their sin, and I will hold you accountable for their blood. But if you do warn the wicked person to turn from their ways and they do not do so, they will die for their sin, though you yourself will be saved."
> (Ezek. 33:1-9)

Third, the phrase "shake the dust off your feet" also announces an unavoidable punishment and judgment, since a refusal to hear and receive the message prevents an opportunity for repentance. When Jesus says, "Truly I tell you, it will be more bearable for Sodom and Gomorrah on the day of judgment than for that town" (Matt. 10:15), He is clearly saying that those who reject the message of repentance will be punished severely.

The Lord was not trying to hide the wrath of God. He pronounces woe on unresponsive and unrepentant towns and uses them as examples of eternal punishment, saying that Sodom's judgment would be less severe than theirs.

> Then Jesus began to denounce the towns in which most of his miracles had been performed, because they did not repent. "Woe to you, Chorazin! Woe to you, Bethsaida! For if the miracles that were performed in you had been performed in Tyre and Sidon, they would have repented long ago in sackcloth and ashes. But I tell you, it will be more bearable for Tyre and Sidon on the day of judgment than for you. And you, Capernaum, will you be lifted to the heavens? No, you will go down to Hades. For if the miracles that were performed in you had been performed in Sodom, it would have remained to this day. But I tell you that it will be more bearable for Sodom on the day of judgment than for you."
> (Matt. 11:20-24)

THE UTOPIA OF A STRANGE LOVE

"Woe to you" speaks not only of the Lord's dissatisfaction but to judgment, sorrow, grief, and the threat of losing one's life. When Jesus uses the phrase, He pronounces direct judgment in the coming wrath of God. In diagnosing the spiritual leaders in Israel in Matthew 23, Jesus uses "woe" eight times. John MacArthur says,

> Here you have a rather pitiful pronunciation of doom on spiritual phonies who masquerade as if they are spiritual leaders when, in fact, they are not at all spiritual leaders. . . . When Jesus says woe, woe, woe all these times, this is not a wish; this is the statement of a fact. His condemnations here are factual, not wishful. It isn't like people today who might say, "Well curse you," which seems to be a rather popular phrase. It is not just a wish that you be cursed; it is a fact. It is a statement of absolute fact. Divine judgment is set in motion when Jesus says you are cursed. That is not a wish, that is a fact.[63]

If Jesus pronounced woes against the false leaders of that day, the mind could only imagine His words for today's wolves dressed in shepherds' clothing!

The Parables and Pragmatism

There are over thirty parables in the New Testament. All are gospel centered, and many refer to God's wrath or eternal destruction. In our day, the parables have taken a spiritual beating by a self-absorbed culture, which reduces them to stories that can fit anyone's imagination. They are even used to justify why we need to be creative and to use stories in our preaching today. After all, if Jesus used stories to reach His generation, why not us? Jesus, a Master of pedagogy teaching, has been replaced by a Jesus who only wants to motivate people by narrating inspirational tales. This has become the method of choice to reach today's generation.

What many fail to discern is that this methodology has been Satan's Trojan Horse throughout the ages to get inside the church and subvert it from within. The Church Growth Movement—the new school of

---

63. John MacArthur, *The Condemnation of False Spiritual Leaders*, Part 3 (March 18, 1984).

evangelism—boasts that their "new" methods are more effective than the traditional methods. Their focus is on converting "homogenous units" and downplaying traditional doctrinal teaching and preaching. In 1969 Martyn Lloyd-Jones prophetically saw this movement on the horizon and warned against it in his day. He proclaimed that marketing ideas and strategies, and current trends, are not anything new or fresh. They are old, and they will eventually end in failure:

> The moment you begin to turn from preaching to these other expedients you will find yourself undergoing a constant series of changes. One of the advantages of being old is that you have experience, so when something new comes up, and you see people getting very excited about it, you happen to be in the position of being able to remember a similar excitement perhaps forty years ago. And so one has seen fashions and vogues and stunts coming one after another in the Church. Each one creates great excitement and enthusiasm and is loudly advertised as the thing that is going to fill the churches, the thing that is going to solve the problem. They have said that about every single one of them. But in a few years they have forgotten all about it, and another stunt comes along, or another new idea; somebody has hit upon the one thing needful or he has a psychological understanding of modern man. Here is the thing, and everybody rushes after it; but soon it wanes and disappears and something else takes its place. This is, surely, a very sad and regrettable state for the Christian Church to be in, that like the world she should exhibit these constant changes of fashion. In that state she lacks the stability and the solidity and the continuing message that has ever been the glory of the Christian Church. . . . These proposals that we should preach less, and do various other things more, are of course not new at all. People seem to think that all this is quite new, and that it is the hallmark of modernity to decry or to depreciate preaching, and to put your emphasis on these

other things. The simple answer to that is that there is nothing new about it.[64]

When the end justifies the means, pragmatism rules the day. Pragmatism is now the leading or guiding principle of how to do ministry, and its view of the church's primary function is eternally flawed. Biblical truths and scriptural accuracy take a back seat to what is "working." When pragmatism becomes the measuring tool of truth and success, the church is sedated under demonic anesthesia. The dangerous thing is that this approach appears to work. Attendance figures have increased in many churches. Multiple satellite campus are established. Money has increased in the coffers. In fact, megachurches have been overrun by the prosperity gospel, which preaches that God's favor is proved in material wealth. Forthrightly, the prosperity gospel only appeals to a culture that covets the American dream.

The flip side of this is that people are not growing due to a lack of biblical maturity. Without spiritual growth, there is a lack of spiritual discernment. There is no attaining to the whole measure of the fullness of Christ, as Paul warned.

> Until we all reach unity in the faith and in the knowledge of the Son of God and become mature, attaining to the whole measure of the fullness of Christ. Then we will no longer be infants, tossed back and forth by the waves, and blown here and there by every wind of teaching and by the cunning and craftiness of people in their deceitful scheming. Instead, speaking the truth in love, we will grow to become in every respect the mature body of him who is the head, that is, Christ. From him the whole body, joined and held together by every supporting ligament, grows and builds itself up in love, as each part does its work. (Eph. 4:13-16)

These methods can add numbers, but they cannot produce sound discipleship. They can draw crowds, but they cannot develop biblical worldview mindsets. We must remember that not all growth is healthy; it also could be a sign of a deadly infection. Only sound doctrine can develop a healthy spiritual life in believers. The apostle Paul used the word *sound* nine

---

64. Martyn Lloyd-Jones, *Preaching and Preachers* (Grand Rapids: Zondervan, 1971), 35.

times in the pastoral Epistles—1 Timothy, 2 Timothy, and Titus. In the Greek, it is *hugiaino*, and it is where we get our English word *hygiene*. It means that which causes good health is wholesome, complete, and without error. It refers to teaching that gives spiritual health to the inner man. It denotes to teaching which individuals could build and place their lives upon. In the context of sound doctrine, *hugiaino* refers to Christians whose beliefs and thoughts are free from a mixture of deceit. When sound doctrine is applied, it produces sound conduct and correct behavior in the lives of believers. When methodology trumps theology, however, clever storytelling is considered God's medicine for a narcissist generation. Did Jesus design parables to meet the demand of seekers? Was this why He started telling stories? After several years of forthright teaching, was Jesus now changing His method in order to draw and please the crowds?

The Purpose of Parables

When using parables, Jesus always shared graphic analogies, such as the master and his servant, the lost sheep, the dishonest steward, and so on. The meaning of the stories was clear in the context of His teaching—but not to all. The parables were a new and different way to share spiritual principles, and their original purpose stood in sharp contrast to the way parables are used today. The reason for this is that when Jesus taught in stories, His intention was to *conceal* and not to *reveal* the truth. Because many of the parables illustrated the coming of God's wrath, they acted in essence as the judgment of God. After Jesus told the disciples the parable of the sower, they asked Him to explain why He was teaching this way.

> The disciples came to him and asked, "Why do you speak to the people in parables?" He replied, "Because the knowledge of the secrets of the kingdom of heaven has been given to you, but not to them. Whoever has will be given more, and they will have an abundance. Whoever does not have, even what they have will be taken from them. This is why I speak to them in parables: 'Though seeing, they do not see; though hearing, they do not hear or understand.' In them is fulfilled the prophecy of Isaiah: 'You will be ever hearing but never understanding; you will be ever seeing but never perceiving. For this people's heart has become calloused; they hardly

THE UTOPIA OF A STRANGE LOVE

hear with their ears, and they have closed their eyes. Otherwise they might see with their eyes, hear with their ears, understand with their hearts and turn, and I would heal them.' But blessed are your eyes because they see, and your ears because they hear." (Matt. 13:10-16)

Until the Lord began using parables, He always spoke clearly and candidly. What led Him to change His standard format? Perhaps His patience had been tested to its limits with the spiritual leaders' persistent rejection of His teaching and the signs that followed. Scripture tells us God's Spirit will not always strive with men. The Lord said, "My Spirit will not contend with humans forever" (Gen. 6:3). No doubt, Jesus was angry with the leaders' blasphemy against the Spirit: "Whoever is not with me is against me, and whoever does not gather with me scatters. And so I tell you, every kind of sin and slander can be forgiven, but blasphemy against the Spirit will not be forgiven" (Matt. 12:30-31). In any event, the parables were not designed to make the truth clear. They were meant to hide the truth from those who refuse to believe.

Parables teach the judgment of God intermingled with the mercy of God. When Jesus used parables, He did it to withhold truth from unbelievers, thus removing the responsibility and accountability for obeying that truth. At the same time, however, He withheld truth as judgment, and as such He removed the element of the Holy Spirit's conviction to change one's behavior. Once again, we see the love of God intermingled with the wrath of God. Modish church leaders who think we should do away with dogmatic doctrinal preaching and tell stories "like Jesus did" because "this is how we are going to win this generation" clearly are not being led by the Spirit and have no knowledge or understanding about the true meaning of the parables. How long did Jesus continue with this style? "Jesus spoke all these things to the crowd in parables; he did not say anything to them without using a parable" (Matt. 13:34). For the rest of His Galilean ministry, when speaking in public, Jesus only used stories. We will look closely at two of them.

The Parable of the Wicked Tenants

Matthew's Gospel records many important events leading up to the parable of the wicked tenants, which appears in chapter twenty-one (it is also called the parable of the wicked vinedressers). In order to understand this parable fully, let us look at some of the events.

We begin with Jesus' final week before the Crucifixion. We are told that "Early in the morning, as Jesus was on his way back to the city, he was hungry. Seeing a fig tree by the road, he went up to it but found nothing on it except leaves. Then he said to it, 'May you never bear fruit again!' Immediately the tree withered" (Matt. 21:18-19). The fig tree was often used in scripture as a symbol for Israel. As a divine act of God's judgment on earthly Israel's spiritual fruitlessness, the Lord curses the fig tree. From a distance, this tree must have showed great promise, but upon closer inspection, it was found wanting. The fig tree (Israel) was therefore cursed for its neglected advantages and its hypocrisy. This story of the fig tree was a presage of the judgment coming to the nation of Israel—a warning of what the future holds.

Then Jesus entered and cleansed the temple:

> Jesus entered the temple courts and drove out all who were buying and selling there. He overturned the tables of the money changers and the benches of those selling doves. "It is written," he said to them, "'My house will be called a house of prayer,' but you are making it 'a den of robbers.'" The blind and the lame came to him at the temple, and he healed them. But when the chief priests and the teachers of the law saw the wonderful things he did and the children shouting in the temple courts, "Hosanna to the Son of David," they were indignant. "Do you hear what these children are saying?" they asked him. "Yes," replied Jesus, "have you never read, 'From the lips of children and infants you, Lord, have called forth your praise'?" And he left them and went out of the city to Bethany, where he spent the night. (Matt. 21:12-17)

What Jesus did was more than just "cleansing" the temple. He forcibly drove out those who were buying and selling there. The Greek word is *ekballō*, meaning to command one or to cause one to depart in haste, or to lead one away with an irresistible force. Church leaders should take note. When the Judge of heaven stamps His eviction order, there is no power on earth that can restrain His decision. "His dominion is an eternal dominion; his kingdom endures from generation to generation. All the peoples of the

THE UTOPIA OF A STRANGE LOVE

earth are regarded as nothing. He does as he pleases with the powers of heaven and the peoples of the earth. No one can hold back his hand or say to him: 'What have you done?'" (Dan. 4: 34-35).

We see in the very next thing that happens, when Jesus and His disciples pass by the fig tree that Jesus curses, the swiftness of judgment approaching the nation of Israel when the tree withers. After this, "Jesus entered the temple courts, and, while he was teaching, the chief priests and the elders of the people came to him. 'By what authority are you doing these things?' they asked. 'And who gave you this authority?'" (Matt. 21:23). Jesus answers the question of the chief priests by first asking one of His own: "Jesus replied, 'I will also ask you one question. If you answer me, I will tell you by what authority I am doing these things. John's baptism—where did it come from? Was it from heaven, or of human origin?' They discussed it among themselves and said, 'If we say, "From heaven," he will ask, "Then why didn't you believe him?" But if we say, "Of human origin"—we are afraid of the people, for they all hold that John was a prophet.' So they answered Jesus, 'We don't know'" (Matt. 21:24-27).

The chief priests and the elders wanted to have Jesus' answer so they could trap Him, but Jesus puts the shoe on the other foot. His question traps and places them in a real dilemma. If they affirmed John the Baptist's ministry, then ultimately they would condemn themselves by rejecting Jesus' ministry. The same source that approved John was the same source that approves Jesus. This is why they answered, "We don't know." This exchange caused the leaders to become angry and put them in greater conflict with Jesus.

Jesus further frustrated the leaders by telling three parables: the parable of the two sons, the parable of the wicked tenants, and the parable of the marriage feast. The parable of the two sons was the "appetizer":

> What do you think? There was a man who had two sons. He went to the first and said, "Son, go and work today in the vineyard." "I will not," he answered, but later he changed his mind and went. Then the father went to the other son and said the same thing. He answered, "I will, sir," but he did not go. Which of the two did what his father wanted? "The first," they answered. Jesus said to them, "Truly I tell you, the tax collectors and the prostitutes are entering the kingdom of God ahead of you. For John came to you to show you the

THE SERMON ON THE MOUNT

way of righteousness, and you did not believe him, but the tax collectors and the prostitutes did. And even after you saw this, you did not repent and believe him" (Matt. 21:28-32).

Jesus continued His confrontation with the chief priests and elders for being hypocrites and religious frauds by telling the parable of the two sons who were sent to work in the vineyard. The parable illustrated the hypocrisy and deceit of the scribes and Pharisees, who pretended to be righteous workers but were in fact full of disbelief. The worst sinners were preferable to them.

The parable of the two sons sets the stage for the next two parables—the one of the wicked tenants and the one of the marriage feast. But this parable came first because Jesus wanted the leaders to testify against themselves. He told them the very people they thought were doomed would enter the kingdom of God before them. "Truly I tell you, the tax collectors and the prostitutes are entering the kingdom of God ahead of you. For John came to you to show you the way of righteousness, and you did not believe him, but the tax collectors and the prostitutes did. And even after you saw this, you did not repent and believe him" (Matt. 21:31-32). Those remarks caused the leaders' blood to boil, but Jesus was only getting started. Now that they had verbally condemned themselves by their own admission, Jesus condemned them for their actions.

The parable of the wicked tenants climaxed the hostility against Jesus and Israel's spiritual leaders:

> Listen to another parable: There was a landowner who planted a vineyard. He put a wall around it, dug a winepress in it and built a watchtower. Then he rented the vineyard to some farmers and moved to another place. When the harvest time approached, he sent his servants to the tenants to collect his fruit. The tenants seized his servants; they beat one, killed another, and stoned a third. Then he sent other servants to them, more than the first time, and the tenants treated them the same way. Last of all, he sent his son to them. "They will respect my son," he said. But when the tenants saw the son, they said to each other, "This is the heir. Come, let's kill him and take his inheritance." So they took him and threw him out of the vineyard and killed him.

THE UTOPIA OF A STRANGE LOVE

> Therefore, when the owner of the vineyard comes, what will he do to those tenants? "He will bring those wretches to a wretched end," they replied, "and he will rent the vineyard to other tenants, who will give him his share of the crop at harvest time." Jesus said to them, "Have you never read in the Scriptures: 'The stone the builders rejected has become the cornerstone; the Lord has done this, and it is marvelous in our eyes'? Therefore I tell you that the kingdom of God will be taken away from you and given to a people who will produce its fruit. Anyone who falls on this stone will be broken to pieces; anyone on whom it falls will be crushed." When the chief priests and the Pharisees heard Jesus' parables, they knew he was talking about them. They looked for a way to arrest him, but they were afraid of the crowd because the people held that he was a prophet. (Matt. 21:33-46)

This parable is both historical and prophetic. It is historical because in it Jesus tells the history of Israel from God's point of view. It is prophetic because the Lord revealed precisely what was going to happen to the nation of Israel when its Jewish leadership rejected the Son of God. The lack of obedience on the part of Israel's religious leaders meant that kingdom responsibilities would be inherited by the Gentiles. Their opportunity was forfeit.

The landlord in this parable represents God, and the vineyard itself represents Israel. Jesus used familiar imagery from the Hebrew scripture that the Jewish leaders would not have missed. The song of the vineyard appears in the fifth chapter of Isaiah: "I will sing for the one I love a song about his vineyard: My loved one had a vineyard on a fertile hillside. . . . The vineyard of the Lord Almighty is the nation of Israel, and the people of Judah are the vines he delighted in. And he looked for justice, but saw bloodshed; for righteousness, but heard cries of distress" (Isa. 5:1, 7). The Lord developed His vineyard with great care and with all of the necessary preparations so it would be successful. The vinedressers would be without excuse. The landlord leased out the vineyard to the vinedressers—the Jewish spiritual leaders—to maintain and oversee his property. When harvest time came, the landlord sent his servants—the Old Testament prophets—to reap his portion of the fruit. But the tenants beat one of the servants, killed one, and stoned another. The landowner sent additional servants, more than the first time, and the tenants treated them the same way.

After his servants were rejected, the landowner took a more drastic action when "last of all, he sent his son to them. 'They will respect my son,' he said." But when the tenants saw the son, they recognized their chance to secure the vineyard for themselves. "They said to each other, 'This is the heir. Come, let's kill him and take his inheritance.' So they took him and threw him out of the vineyard and killed him." At that time, the law provided that if there were no heirs, the property would pass to those in possession. This plan clearly was premeditated murder, set in motion by the Jewish leadership.

Throughout the ages, God showed great love and patience to His chosen people by sending His prophets to guide them. Yet His care and concern was commonly met with mockery and scorn. "The Lord, the God of their ancestors, sent word to them through his messengers again and again, because he had pity on his people and on his dwelling place. But they mocked God's messengers, despised his words and scoffed at his prophets until the wrath of the Lord was aroused against his people and there was no remedy" (2 Chron. 36:15-16). When Jesus asked, "When the owner of the vineyard comes, what will he do to those tenants?" we see that God's forbearance is indeed beyond human comprehension, but when He is ready to respond, no one can reverse His decision. We need to be careful of leaders who misinterpret God's delay in judgment by suggesting He is too merciful to judge.

Jesus' question, "When the owner of the vineyard comes, what will he do to those tenants?" forces to the religious leaders to declare their own fate. They say, "He will bring those wretches to a wretched end . . . and he will rent the vineyard to other tenants, who will give him his share of the crop at harvest time." The scribes and Pharisees agreed that the landowner's wrath would be just and the tenants' punishment deserved. Jesus had been speaking to Israel's past and present disobedience, but at this point in the parable, He deals with Israel's future. That future includes the grave consequences of rejecting Him as Messiah: "Have you never read in the Scriptures: 'The stone the builders rejected has become the cornerstone; the Lord has done this, and it is marvelous in our eyes'? Therefore I tell you that the kingdom of God will be taken away from you and given to a people who will produce its fruit. Anyone who falls on this stone will be broken to pieces;

THE UTOPIA OF A STRANGE LOVE

anyone on whom it falls will be crushed" (Matt. 21:42-44). Jesus' words of judgment were scathing and more than what the leaders could endure: "When the chief priests and the Pharisees heard Jesus' parables, they knew he was talking about them. They looked for a way to arrest him, but they were afraid of the crowd because the people held that he was a prophet" (Matt. 21:45-46).

Jesus reminded the chief priests and the Pharisees that their rejection of Him had been recorded since time past and that their rejection would not change who He is. He quoted the messianic psalm, "The stone the builders rejected has become the cornerstone; the Lord has done this, and it is marvelous in our eyes. The Lord has done it this very day; let us rejoice today and be glad" (Ps. 118:22-24). In spite of their approval or disapproval, Jesus was and is the chief cornerstone! Since He is the chief cornerstone, the main piece of God's salvific foundation, He has ultimate authority over human affairs.

The consequence of the Lord's judgment against the Jewish religious leaders was that the kingdom of God would be taken away from them and given to believing Gentiles who had been grafted into the gospel. "Therefore I tell you that the kingdom of God will be taken away from you and given to a people who will produce its fruit" (Matt. 21:43). Predictably, the verdict was not well received from the leaders; their anger and hostility increased, setting the stage for the next parable of the marriage feast.

The Parable of the Marriage Feast

Jesus spoke to them again in parables, saying: "The kingdom of heaven is like a king who prepared a wedding banquet for his son. He sent his servants to those who had been invited to the banquet to tell them to come, but they refused to come. Then he sent some more servants and said, 'Tell those who have been invited that I have prepared my dinner: My oxen and fattened cattle have been butchered, and everything is ready. Come to the wedding banquet.' But they paid no attention and went off—one to his field, another to his business. The rest seized his servants, mistreated them and killed them. The king was enraged. He sent his army and destroyed those murderers and burned their city. Then he said to his servants, 'The wedding banquet is ready, but those I invited did not deserve to come. So go to the street corners and invite to the banquet anyone you find.' So the servants went out into the streets and gathered all the people they could find, the bad as well as the good, and the wedding hall was filled with guests. But when the king came in to see the guests, he noticed a man there who was not wearing wedding clothes. He asked, 'How did you get in here without wedding clothes, friend?' The man was speechless. Then the king told the attendants, 'Tie him hand and foot, and throw him outside, into the darkness, where there will be weeping and gnashing of teeth.' For many are invited, but few are chosen." Then the Pharisees went out and laid plans to trap him in his words. (Matt. 22:1-14)

As the confrontation between Jesus and the leaders of Israel escalates, Jesus tells a story revealing the fate of the nation and the leaders. It is a story of a marriage feast, which is usually a great time of celebration and joy in the Jewish culture. In this story, however, the marriage feast becomes a time of regret and pain. Before we dissect the parable, it is important to know some things concerning a Jewish wedding in Jesus' day.

When a young Jewish man wanted to take a wife, he prepared a marriage covenant, which he then presented to both the young woman and her father. This covenant, or contract, included a bride price meant to compensate the woman's parents for the cost of raising her. The wedding itself was arranged by the father of the groom working with the father of the bride to determine the date and place of the ceremony. Before that, however, the young man would announce to his bride-to-be, "I am going to prepare a place for you," and "I will return for you when everything is ready." Usually, he would then prepare a room for their honeymoon in his father's house. When the home was ready, the groom would return for his bride without notice. Finally, the marriage ceremony would then take place, and the wedding banquet would follow. Whereas a few are invited to the wedding ceremony, many others are invited to the marriage feast to celebrate the marriage of the son.

In the parable of the marriage feast, the king arranges a wedding for his son. He sent his servants out to call those who were invited to the wedding, but everyone rejected the invitation and refused to attend. In telling

THE UTOPIA OF A STRANGE LOVE

this story, Jesus highlights their rejection and stubbornness. The king sent more servants to invite others to the marriage feast. The very God the religious leaders proclaim they know is treated trivially, and the invitees carry on with their own interests. "They paid no attention and went off—one to his field, another to his business. The rest seized his servants, mistreated them and killed them" (Matt. 22:5-6). They were so preoccupied with their lives that they had little concern for the king's desires. They treated him and his servants in the worst possible way, and their behavior provoked the king to become furious. A third invitation is now given for the king's servants to invite those who previously were not invited, because those who have rejected the king were no longer found worthy. "The wedding banquet is ready, but those I invited did not deserve to come. So go to the street corners and invite to the banquet anyone you find" (Matt. 22:8-9).

When the third group of invitees gathered for the wedding banquet, the king saw a man there without proper attire, and this troubled him greatly—so much so that he, the king, told the attendants, "Tie him hand and foot, and throw him outside, into the darkness, where there will be weeping and gnashing of teeth. For many are invited, but few are chosen" (Matt. 22:13-14). In that culture, one was expected to wear the proper attire for a wedding banquet. Because these guests were gathered quickly, without time to prepare, the king himself would have supplied the proper garments for the occasion. For this man to be dressed in inappropriate attire indicates he intentionally rejected the king's provision. His selfish decision was an insult to the king, and it was without excuse.

There is a very familiar verse in John's Gospel, a verse that many people quote and some even hold up on poster board during football games. The verse is thrown around so haphazardly that it virtually has lost its meaning. In the Gospel of John, after Jesus revealed to Nicodemus how spiritually bankrupt he was, He taught on the true meaning of salvation:

> Very truly I tell you, we speak of what we know, and we testify to what we have seen, but still you people do not accept our testimony. I have spoken to you of earthly things and you do not believe; how then will you believe if I speak of heavenly things? No one has ever gone into heaven except the one who came from heaven—the Son of Man. Just as Moses lifted up the snake in the wilderness, so the Son of Man must be lifted up, that everyone who believes may have

eternal life in him. For God so loved the world that he gave his one and only Son, that whoever believes in him shall not perish but have eternal life. For God did not send his Son into the world to condemn the world, but to save the world through him. Whoever believes in him is not condemned, but whoever does not believe stands condemned already because they have not believed in the name of God's one and only Son. This is the verdict: Light has come into the world, but people loved darkness instead of light because their deeds were evil. Everyone who does evil hates the light, and will not come into the light for fear that their deeds will be exposed. But whoever lives by the truth comes into the light, so that it may be seen plainly that what they have done has been done in the sight of God. (John 3:11-21)

The frequently-quoted verse I mentioned appears in this block of scripture. It is John 3:16: "For God so loved the world that he gave his one and only Son, that whoever believes in him shall not perish but have eternal life." This is indeed a lovely and powerful verse, but when examined in context, we see that God's love for humankind is demonstrated in that He gave His Son as the sacrifice for our sin. God loves the world not because we deserved it, or because we were worth it. His love is based on His own will, which He has purposed for Himself. God's love is based on His own glory.

Notice in the text that God loved the world so much "that he gave his one and only Son, that whoever believes in him shall not perish but have eternal life." This is a conditional promise. Contrary to what many believe and teach, the word *world* does not mean the elect—those who are already predestined to be saved; the word is applying to all humankind. It's highly important that we approach the Word of God without presupposed notions. Reading our personal or preferred preacher interpretation into a scripture text is not only dangerous but it's dishonest. Rediscovering the true biblical meaning of atonement and election is needed more than ever.

Moreover, this promise is conditioned on whether or not someone actually *believes*. When belief in Christ is not present, people will perish. Jesus' discourse follows the same pattern as the theme in the parables. If one believes, eternal life is theirs. If one rejects Christ, however, promised damnation awaits. The Greek word for perish is *apollymi*. It means to destroy,

THE UTOPIA OF A STRANGE LOVE

to be put out of the way entirely, and to be given over to eternal misery in hell. The same verse that speaks about God's love also speaks of His wrath. No eternal doom awaits those who trust in Jesus, but those who refuse to believe have already been tried and condemned. As John records, "Whoever believes in him is not condemned, but whoever does not believe stands condemned already because they have not believed in the name of God's one and only Son. This is the verdict: Light has come into the world, but people loved darkness instead of light because their deeds were evil" (John 3:18-19).

The third chapter of John ends with a heart-wrenching truth: "Whoever believes in the Son has eternal life, but whoever rejects the Son will not see life, for God's wrath remains on them" (John 3:36). The truth is that we were already under God's wrath before we repented and surrendered to Christ as Lord. This is why the gospel is called the "Good News." The bad news is that we were enemies with God, and therefore His wrath was upon us. The apostle Paul explained it this way: "For if, while we were God's enemies, we were reconciled to him through the death of his Son, how much more, having been reconciled, shall we be saved through his life!" (Rom. 5:10). And, "Once you were alienated from God and were enemies in your minds because of your evil behavior" (Col. 1:21). Yet God's love for us was demonstrated in that He sent His only begotten Son, who is the only perfect and acceptable sacrifice, to move men and women from death to life, from darkness to light. This is indeed the best of news!

With this background, we now have a better understanding of the purpose of the parables. In the parables we have reviewed, we see God's love and grace on the same playing field as His wrath. God's wrath is evidenced when men and women reject His plan of salvation: "Whoever believes in him is not condemned, but whoever does not believe stands condemned already because they have not believed in the name of God's one and only Son" (John 3:18). It is a reaction based on the response of people: "Light has come into the world, but people loved darkness instead of light because their deeds were evil" (John 3:19). It is clear that Jesus spoke often about judgment and condemnation. Let us now examine what the apostle Paul said about the topic of God's wrath.

THE APOSTLE PAUL

The Epistle from Paul to the Christians in Rome is more formal than the other letters Paul wrote. It is a doctrinal work, set forth in a systematic way. In fact, this letter is the most systematic presentation of theology found anywhere in the scriptures. Even Christian leaders who abhor dogmatic teaching use the letter to the Romans to preach and teach about grace. Maybe this is why the grace message frequently used today is biblically misrepresented. How can one speak about grace and neglect the other doctrinal matters that make grace what it is? The book of Romans discusses a number of essential Christian doctrinal truths, including original sin, justification by faith, sanctification, the meaning of the Cross, propitiation, Christian liberty, and the believer's relationship to civil authority.

One doctrinal truth not as widely discussed as the others is Paul's treatment of the wrath of God. It is the wrath of God that sets the stage for the meaning of other truths. Paul speaks of a wrath that is present and a wrath that is to come when he states, "because of your stubbornness and your unrepentant heart, you are storing up wrath against yourself for the day of God's wrath, when his righteous judgment will be revealed" (Rom. 2:5). Paul begins with a view of human sin, declaring that all men and women are under the wrath of God and in desperate need of God's righteousness: "For in the gospel the righteousness of God is revealed—a righteousness that is by faith from first to last, just as it is written: 'The righteous will live by faith'" (Rom. 1:17). Paul also states, "The wrath of God is being revealed from heaven against all the godlessness and wickedness of people, who suppress the truth by their wickedness" (Rom. 1:18).

Humanity is under the wrath of God due to the suppression of the truth. The Greek word for suppress is *katechō*, and it means to hold back or to hold down. We are all under the wrath of God because of our holding back faith and rejecting His Word in favor of our own sin. In Romans Paul displays the necessity for us to flee from God's righteous wrath by turning to His Good News. And what is the Good News? It is the gospel that while our sin debt is too high for any of us to pay the bill, God sent His Son to pay for our sins.

THE UTOPIA OF A STRANGE LOVE

The Lamb of God

Jesus, the Lamb of God, was the perfect sacrifice for the sins of the world. John the Baptist mentions this same expression: "The next day John saw Jesus coming toward him and said, 'Look, the Lamb of God, who takes away the sin of the world!'" (John 1:29). The term *Lamb of God* had great significance dating back to the Old Testament. At the time of the Israelites' exodus from Egypt, God told Moses and the Jewish people to select a lamb from among their flock which would be known as the Passover lamb:

> The Lord said to Moses and Aaron in Egypt, "This month is to be for you the first month, the first month of your year. Tell the whole community of Israel that on the tenth day of this month each man is to take a lamb for his family, one for each household. If any household is too small for a whole lamb, they must share one with their nearest neighbor, having taken into account the number of people there are. You are to determine the amount of lamb needed in accordance with what each person will eat. The animals you choose must be year-old males without defect, and you may take them from the sheep or the goats. Take care of them until the fourteenth day of the month, when all the members of the community of Israel must slaughter them at twilight. Then they are to take some of the blood and put it on the sides and tops of the doorframes of the houses where they eat the lambs. That same night they are to eat the meat roasted over the fire, along with bitter herbs, and bread made without yeast. Do not eat the meat raw or boiled in water, but roast it over a fire—with the head, legs and internal organs. Do not leave any of it till morning; if some is left till morning, you must burn it. This is how you are to eat it: with your cloak tucked into your belt, your sandals on your feet and your staff in your hand. Eat it in haste; it is the Lord's Passover. On that same night I will pass through Egypt and strike down every firstborn of both people and animals, and I will bring judgment on all the gods of Egypt. I am the Lord. The blood will be a sign for you on the houses where you are, and when I see the blood, I will pass over you. No

destructive plague will touch you when I strike Egypt. This is a day you are to commemorate; for the generations to come you shall celebrate it as a festival to the Lord—a lasting ordinance. For seven days you are to eat bread made without yeast. On the first day remove the yeast from your houses, for whoever eats anything with yeast in it from the first day through the seventh must be cut off from Israel. On the first day hold a sacred assembly, and another one on the seventh day. Do no work at all on these days, except to prepare food for everyone to eat; that is all you may do. Celebrate the Festival of Unleavened Bread, because it was on this very day that I brought your divisions out of Egypt. Celebrate this day as a lasting ordinance for the generations to come. In the first month you are to eat bread made without yeast, from the evening of the fourteenth day until the evening of the twenty-first day. For seven days no yeast is to be found in your houses. And anyone, whether foreigner or native-born, who eats anything with yeast in it must be cut off from the community of Israel. Eat nothing made with yeast. Wherever you live, you must eat unleavened bread." Then Moses summoned all the elders of Israel and said to them, "Go at once and select the animals for your families and slaughter the Passover lamb. Take a bunch of hyssop, dip it into the blood in the basin and put some of the blood on the top and on both sides of the doorframe. None of you shall go out of the door of your house until morning. When the Lord goes through the land to strike down the Egyptians, he will see the blood on the top and sides of the doorframe and will pass over that doorway, and he will not permit the destroyer to enter your houses and strike you down. Obey these instructions as a lasting ordinance for you and your descendants. When you enter the land that the Lord will give you as he promised, observe this ceremony. And when your children ask you, 'What does this ceremony mean to you?' then tell them, 'It is the Passover sacrifice to the Lord, who passed over the houses of the Israelites in Egypt and spared our homes when he struck down the

THE UTOPIA OF A STRANGE LOVE

Egyptians.'" Then the people bowed down and worshiped. The Israelites did just what the Lord commanded Moses and Aaron. (Exod. 12:1-28)

The Passover lamb was not just any lamb; this one had to be a male lamb of the first year and completely without blemish. It had to be slain in public, and the blood from the slain lamb was to be posted on the doorposts as a sign for God to protect and not destroy the first born of the household. The Lamb of God described by the prophet Isaiah clearly connects the Lamb of God with Jesus Christ, the promised Messiah:

> Surely he took up our pain and bore our suffering, yet we considered him punished by God, stricken by him, and afflicted. But he was pierced for our transgressions, he was crushed for our iniquities; the punishment that brought us peace was on him, and by his wounds we are healed. We all, like sheep, have gone astray, each of us has turned to our own way; and the Lord has laid on him the iniquity of us all. He was oppressed and afflicted, yet he did not open his mouth; he was led like a lamb to the slaughter, and as a sheep before its shearers is silent, so he did not open his mouth. By oppression and judgment he was taken away. Yet who of his generation protested? For he was cut off from the land of the living; for the transgression of my people he was punished. . . . Yet it was the Lord's will to crush him and cause him to suffer, and though the Lord makes his life an offering for sin, he will see his offspring and prolong his days, and the will of the Lord will prosper in his hand. After he has suffered, he will see the light of life and be satisfied; by his knowledge my righteous servant will justify many, and he will bear their iniquities. Therefore I will give him a portion among the great, and he will divide the spoils with the strong, because he poured out his life unto death, and was numbered with the transgressors. For he bore the sin of many, and made intercession for the transgressors. (Isa. 53:4-8, 10-12)

In 1 Corinthians Paul writes that we should "get rid of the old yeast, so that you may be a new unleavened batch—as you really are. For Christ, our Passover lamb, has been sacrificed" (1 Cor. 5:7). And the apostle Peter declared that Jesus was "a lamb without blemish or defect" (1 Pet. 1:19). What is the connection, then, between Jesus as the Lamb of God and God's wrath?

Atonement/Propitiation

Another doctrinal truth found in Paul's book of Romans is the doctrine of atonement, from which we receive the theological term *propitiation*. Simply put, propitiation means the appeasement or satisfaction of God's wrath against sin. Unfortunately, this teaching has become one of the most overlooked doctrines in the church today. The strange love the church has embraced has subverted this essential truth and weakened our understanding of the work of Christ at the Cross. This has indeed become the adversary's plan. If Christ's salvation work is cheapened by a distorted grace and lack of understanding of the true purpose of the Cross, then how can men really be saved? Paul writes,

> For all have sinned and fall short of the glory of God, and all are justified freely by his grace through the redemption that came by Christ Jesus. God presented Christ as a sacrifice of atonement, through the shedding of his blood—to be received by faith. He did this to demonstrate his righteousness, because in his forbearance he had left the sins committed beforehand unpunished—he did it to demonstrate his righteousness at the present time, so as to be just and the one who justifies those who have faith in Jesus. Where, then, is boasting? It is excluded. Because of what law? The law that requires works? No, because of the law that requires faith. For we maintain that a person is justified by faith apart from the works of the law. (Rom. 3:23-28)

The apostle John said that "if anybody does sin, we have an advocate with the Father—Jesus Christ, the Righteous One. He is the atoning sacrifice for our sins, and not only for ours but also for the sins of the whole world" (1 John 2:1-2). He also wrote, "This is love: not that we

THE UTOPIA OF A STRANGE LOVE

loved God, but that he loved us and sent his Son as an atoning sacrifice for our sins" (1 John 4:10). Theologian and author James Montgomery Boice believes the wrath of God is necessary as the only remedy against our sin. He writes that "anyone reading the first three and a half chapters of Romans will clearly see that it is precisely the wrath of God that is our problem. We are under wrath because of sin. Therefore, if the wrath of God cannot be turned aside by someone or in some way, we are lost."[65] In his book *The Cross of Christ*, John Stott said when it comes to reconciling men to God, "the initiative has been taken by God himself in his sheer mercy and grace. . . . This is already clear in the Old Testament, in which the sacrifices were recognized not as human works but as divine gifts. They did not make God gracious; they were provided by a gracious God in order that he might act graciously towards his sinful people."[66]

Leviticus 17:11 tells us, "the life of a creature is in the blood, and I have given it to you to make atonement for yourselves on the altar; it is the blood that makes atonement for one's life." This truth is even more plainly recognized in the main texts about propitiation in the New Testament, where God himself presented Jesus Christ as a propitiatory sacrifice: "God presented Christ as a sacrifice of atonement, through the shedding of his blood—to be received by faith. He did this to demonstrate his righteousness, because in his forbearance he had left the sins committed beforehand unpunished" (Rom. 3:25). "This is love: not that we loved God, but that he loved us and sent his Son as an atoning sacrifice for our sins" (1 John 4:10).

It cannot be emphasized too strongly that God's love is the source, not the consequence, of the atonement. As Scottish theologian P. T. Forsyth expressed it, "The atonement did not procure grace, it flowed from grace."[67] Put another way, God does not love us because Christ died for us; Christ died for us because God loved us. If it is God's wrath that needs to be propitiated, it is God's love that does the propitiating, and the Person God offered was not somebody else—whether a human or an angel, or even His Son considered as somebody distinct from or external to Himself. No, He offered Himself. In giving His Son, He was giving Himself. "It was the Son of God, i.e. God himself . . . God himself gave himself to save us from

---

65. James Montgomery Boice, *Foundations of the Christian Faith: A Comprehensive and Readable Theology* (Downers Grove, IL: InterVarsity Press, 1986).
66. John Stott, *The Cross of Christ* (Downers Grove, IL: InterVarsity Press, 1986), 198.
67. P. T. Forsyth, *The Atonement in Modern Religious Thought*, 64.

himself."[68] J. I. Packer's *Knowing God* says that "the word propitiation is central to the New Testament. . . . The love of God, the taking of human form by the Son, the meaning of the cross, Christ's heavenly intercession, the way of salvation, all are to be explained in terms of it, and any explanation from which the thought of propitiation is missing will be incomplete, and indeed actually misleading, by New Testament standards."[69]

Many Christians cannot remember the last time they heard teaching on propitiation—the satisfaction of God's wrath against sin. Many have never heard the church teach on this doctrine at any time. This is a travesty, and it is especially so when the reason is to appear to the world as loving and less judgmental. This is definitely not a work of the Holy Spirit. The apostle Paul said, "But now in Christ Jesus you who once were far away have been brought near by the blood of Christ" (Eph. 2:13). We were by nature children of wrath, and we must make very sure we do not let anyone deceive us that we can practice sin and still enter the kingdom of Christ. Paul states without apology that God's wrath is upon those who do deceive:

> Follow God's example, therefore, as dearly loved children and walk in the way of love, just as Christ loved us and gave himself up for us as a fragrant offering and sacrifice to God. But among you there must not be even a hint of sexual immorality, or of any kind of impurity, or of greed, because these are improper for God's holy people. Nor should there be obscenity, foolish talk or coarse joking, which are out of place, but rather thanksgiving. For of this you can be sure: No immoral, impure or greedy person—such a person is an idolater—has any inheritance in the kingdom of Christ and of God. Let no one deceive you with empty words, for because of such things God's wrath comes on those who are disobedient. Therefore do not be partners with them. For you were once darkness, but now you are light in the Lord. Live as children of light (for the fruit of the light consists in all goodness, righteousness and truth) and find out what pleases the Lord. Have nothing to do with the fruitless deeds of darkness, but rather expose them. It is shameful even to

---

68. John Stott, *The Cross of Christ*, 172.
69. J. I. Packer, *Knowing God*, 203.

mention what the disobedient do in secret. But everything exposed by the light becomes visible—and everything that is illuminated becomes a light. This is why it is said: "Wake up, sleeper, rise from the dead, and Christ will shine on you." (Eph. 5:1-14)

To saints who were facing tribulations in Thessalonica, Paul encourages them "to wait for his Son from heaven, whom he raised from the dead—Jesus, who rescues us from the coming wrath" (1 Thess. 1:10).

How Sin Is Tolerated

Satan works tirelessly to remove the concept of God's wrath, because when this is accomplished, the sacrifice of Jesus is nullified. If men and women reject the doctrine of the wrath of God, they also reject the holiness of God. But God *is* holy. It is the essence of who He is. If God is not holy, then He cannot be God. When the prophet Isaiah saw the Lord high and lifted up, he heard the angels cry out and he pronounced woe upon himself:

> In the year that King Uzziah died, I saw the Lord, high and exalted, seated on a throne; and the train of his robe filled the temple. Above him were seraphim, each with six wings: With two wings they covered their faces, with two they covered their feet, and with two they were flying. And they were calling to one another: "Holy, holy, holy is the Lord Almighty; the whole earth is full of his glory." At the sound of their voices the doorposts and thresholds shook and the temple was filled with smoke. "Woe to me!" I cried. "I am ruined! For I am a man of unclean lips, and I live among a people of unclean lips, and my eyes have seen the King, the Lord Almighty." (Isa. 6:1-5)

The vision of God's holiness convicted Isaiah of his own unworthiness and deserved judgment. He cried out for God's mercy, and it was granted. If the wrath of God is removed, what would make men and women cry out to be saved? What would they cry out to be saved from? Without an understanding of God's holiness, sin is reduced to something minor and redefined as mere "mistakes" and "shortcomings." It is no longer popular to preach on sin. With the secular climate found even within the church today, we have developed a lower view of sin where it no longer brings God's wrath because it is only a minor failing. But taking sin lightly has damnable consequences.

I heard one popular leader say, "My job is not to preach on sin. That's not what the Holy Spirit wants me to do." I was dumbfounded. Saying something like the leader said is proof the Holy Spirit was not speaking to him; a demonic spirit was instructing him. This man could not discern which voice was speaking to him yet has multiple published books that have sold into the millions. I have heard people tell others not to worry about sin, because "the more sin is present, the more grace is supplied." This is a pure distortion of Paul's writing in Romans chapter five. When people buy into this type of sentiment, sin is tolerated in the name of grace.

It is only when we truly see the holiness, righteousness, and wrath of God that we plead to God for His mercy and grace. I often wonder what would happen if Jonathan Edwards preached his classic sermon, "Sinners in the Hands of an Angry God,"[70] in today's culture. What would the reaction

---

70. Jonathan Edwards, "Sinners in Hands of an Angry God," 1741. A local pastor had invited Edwards to his church because of the lack of change within the people at his church. Edwards preached this message that focuses on the danger of sin, the terrors of being lost, and the horrors of hell. Most of the sermon's text consists of ten considerations: (1) God may cast wicked men into hell at any given moment; (2) The wicked deserve to be cast into hell. (3) The wicked, at this moment, suffer under God's condemnation to hell; (4) The wicked, on earth—at this very moment—suffer the torments of hell. (5) At any moment God shall permit Satan to fall upon the wicked and seize them as his own; (6) If it were not for God's restraints, there are, in the souls of wicked men, hellish principles reigning which, presently, would kindle and flame out into hellfire; (7) Simply because there are not visible means of death before them at any given moment, the wicked should not feel secure; (8) Simply because it is natural to care for oneself or to think that others may care for them, men should not think themselves safe from God's wrath. All that wicked men may do to save themselves from hell's pains shall afford them nothing if they continue to reject Christ. God has never promised to save us from hell, except for those contained in Christ through the covenant of grace; (9) The wicked must not think, simply because they are not physically in hell, that God (in whose hand the wicked now reside) is not—at this very moment—as angry with them as He is with those miserable creatures He is now tormenting in hell, and who—at this very moment—do feel and bear the fierceness of His wrath; (10) Divine justice does not prevent God from destroying the wicked at any moment. Edwards was interrupted many times before finishing the sermon by people moaning and crying out, "What shall I do to be saved?" This message became the foundation of the Great Awakening that founded many of today's Ivy League colleges.

THE UTOPIA OF A STRANGE LOVE

be? In Edwards' day, that sermon was a catalyst for a great spiritual awakening, where many souls turned to God. Today, when the wrath of God is rejected by much of the church (and all of the world), the ideas presented in that sermon would be laughed at. Edwards would be labeled unloving, not Jesus-like, critical, and overly negative. Yet if the concept of the wrath of God is rejected, the death of Jesus on the cross is ineffectual and useless. If the wrath of God no longer exists today, then neither does God's unchangeableness.

God's Immutability

The unchangeableness of God is referred to as His *immutability*. God is incapable of change of any kind—either in duration of life, or in nature, character, will, or happiness. God is immutable in His essence, attributes, and counsels. Considered in the context of God's immutability, God's wrath is not an overblown reaction but rather a part of His perfection. If the wrath of God is removed, hell becomes a false reality. Indubitably, if there is no wrath of God, then there can be no love of God. People who reject language regarding the wrath of God do so because they would rather expound how He is love. But their rejection actually damages the view they claim to profess. Why? Because Christ's atoning sacrifice to satisfy God's wrath is the greatest demonstration of divine love. Scottish theologian and preacher James Denney (1856–1917), in his book *The Death of Christ*, said that "If the propitiatory death of Jesus is eliminated from the love of God, it might be unfair to say that the love of God is robbed of all meaning, but it is certainly robbed of its apostolic meaning."[71]

For this reason Paul begins his entire explanation of the gospel in Romans not with the love of God but with the wrath of God. The love and wrath of God have never been enemies, and they have never contradicted one another:

> But God demonstrates his own love for us in this: While we were still sinners, Christ died for us. Since we have now been justified by his blood, how much more shall we be saved from God's wrath through him! For if, while we were God's

---

71. James Denney, *The Death of Christ* (Grand Rapids: Christian Classics Ethereal Library, 1911), 152.

enemies, we were reconciled to him through the death of his Son, how much more, having been reconciled, shall we be saved through his life! Not only is this so, but we also boast in God through our Lord Jesus Christ, through whom we have now received reconciliation. (Rom. 5:8-11)

The Great Commission

The wrath of God has been revealed historically, presently, and eternally. If in the Cross of Christ we see only the love of God and not His wrath, we have an incomplete view of the gospel, which is the power of God bringing salvation to everyone who believes. An incomplete view of the gospel produces a distorted view of Christ and His work of redemption. Our efforts to fulfill the Great Commission to "make disciples of all nations, baptizing them in the name of the Father and of the Son and of the Holy Spirit, and teaching them to obey everything I have commanded you" (Matt. 28:19-20) are commendable. But in our efforts, have we neglected to proclaim the very means by which sinners are saved? Are we attempting to reach people for God without disclosing all subjects that are about God?

In our ambition to become relevant to a culture quickly fading away, have we altered God's unchangeable way to salvation and replaced it with self-ordained methods? God forbid! Thinking people can be eternally saved apart from the wrath of God is not "God's new way." It is Satan's old way. Telling sinners that God loves them and He is not angry with them and that all they have to do is to repeat a simple prayer to obtain eternal security is not a message from God. Nor is the removal of the idea behind the wrath of God a modern invention. This ploy is "not of this world" and has been crafted and developed among Satan and his demons.

J. I. Packer said this over forty years ago:

> The modern habit throughout the Christian church is to play this subject down. Those who still believe in the wrath of God (not all do) say little about it; perhaps they do not think much about it. To an age which has unashamedly sold itself to the gods of greed, pride, sex and self-will, the Church mumbles on about God's kindness, but says virtually nothing about His judgment. . . . The fact is that the subject of divine wrath has become taboo in modern society, and Christians

THE UTOPIA OF A STRANGE LOVE

by and large have accepted the taboo and conditioned themselves never to raise the matter. [72]

In the words of Charles Spurgeon, "He who does not believe in the wrath of God, and that God will not punish sin, will not believe that He will pardon it through the blood of His Son."[73]

---

72. J. I. Packer, *Knowing God*, 149.
73. Charles Spurgeon, "Noah's Faith, Fear, Obedience, and Salvation," June 1, 1890, message from the Spurgeon Gems website.

Is Love the Greatest?

"Love wins" is a popular phrase that has taken our culture, including the church, by storm. The phrase has been adopted by the masses today after the Supreme Court of the United States ruled on June 26, 2015, in *Obergefell v. Hodges*, that same-sex couples must be allowed to marry no matter where they live. It was an unprecedented victory for gay rights. States now may not deny marriage licenses to same-sex couples, and all states must recognize same-sex couples' existing marriages. After the deeply divided 5-4 decision, "love wins" postings spread like wildfire.

The modern mindset can be fairly stated this way: "Nothing can hinder us from fulfilling our personal gratifications, because at the end of the day, love conquers all." Personally, I have no problem when the world boasts such things. Self-focused statements from those living according to the spirit of this age are to be expected. After all, the apostle Paul wrote,

> As for you, you were dead in your transgressions and sins, in which you used to live when you followed the ways of this world and of the ruler of the kingdom of the air, the spirit who is now at work in those who are disobedient. All of us also lived among them at one time, gratifying the cravings of our flesh and following its desires and thoughts. Like the rest, we were by nature deserving of wrath. . . . So I tell you this, and insist on it in the Lord, that you must no longer live as the Gentiles do, in the futility of their thinking. They are darkened in their understanding and separated from the life of God because of the ignorance that is in them due to the hardening of their hearts. Having lost all sensitivity, they have given themselves over to sensuality so as to indulge in every kind of impurity, and they are full of greed. (Eph. 2:1-3; 4:17-19)

When the church follows the world's leading, however, danger is looming.

We lose our distinctive voice when we parrot the language of a corrupt system. When we define our terms as the world does, we are quickly headed down a slippery slope. The church, the "called out ones," should never allow the world to usurp or define our vocabulary. The church is "the church of the living God, the pillar and foundation of the truth" (1 Tim. 3:15). In essence, we are supposed to be God's mouthpiece of truth. We are called to be a resource and a dispenser of God's truth in an age where truth is fading away. Sadly, the pressure to be popular and accepted has caused many Christians to reject God's way in order to please others. In our quest to become more culturally broad, a significant element of the church has embraced a foreign view of love. Now, it is all about love. There are no absolutes, there is no judging, no discernment, no hell, and no negativity. The hue and cry is, "No perfect people allowed. We are all sinners, so let love reign."

The thirteenth chapter of 1 Corinthians, the so-called "love chapter," has become the centerpiece of this thinking. Paul writes, "And now these three remain: faith, hope and love. But the greatest of these is love" (1 Cor. 13:13). Those who push an extra-biblical view of love hone in on this verse, without seeing it in its context, and conclude that love is supreme. But is love truly the greatest? Let us examine the context of the chapter so we can draw a biblical conclusion.

Rewriting Paul?

Chapters twelve through fourteen in 1 Corinthians offer the background for establishing order in the church at Corinth. Paul was writing to address the lack of order in the church regarding spiritual gifts—especially the gift of tongues. The Christians in Corinth comprised a highly spiritually-gifted church, and the apostle Paul was concerned that the Holy Spirit's gifts operating in the church should not be confused with secular pagan ritual behavior and practices. Therefore, Paul deals with their lack of understanding of the motive and purpose of God's gifts. Because the Corinthians were speaking in tongues in order to exalt and bring attention to themselves, Paul's design is to bring them back to God's original goal of spiritual gifts. To remind the church that gifts without the working of love is meaningless and unprofitable, he writes, "If I speak in the tongues of men or of angels, but do not have love, I am only a resounding gong or a clanging cymbal. If I have the gift of prophecy and can fathom all mysteries and all knowledge, and if I have a faith that can move mountains, but do not have love, I am nothing" (1 Cor. 13:1-2).

Paul then addresses the issue of sacrifice. He says, "If I give all I possess to the poor and give over my body to hardship that I may boast, but do not have love, I gain nothing" (1 Cor. 13:3). This verse cuts right into the heart of what many consider the very evidence of love. Biblical love is a sacrifice, but not all sacrifice is motivated by love. Serving people and being willing to extend a helping hand can create a false impression that you are loving. I can perform works or services, and in God's eye, they could be considered worthless. The Greek word that Paul is using for love is *agape*, which was explained earlier. It has nothing to do with being friendly or being emotional. Agape is not impulsive love; it is decisive. It is not a love void of feelings, but neither is it driven or led by them. Agape is a love that causes one to deny themselves for the sake of others. We see an example of this type of love in the life of Barnabas. Barnabas, who was motivated out of agape, sold his land and brought the money to the church. Scripture says, "Joseph, a Levite from Cyprus, whom the apostles called Barnabas (which means "son of encouragement"), sold a field he owned and brought the money and put it at the apostles' feet" (Acts 4:36-37).

Ananias and Sapphira, on the other hand, were motived by a desire for self-exaltation and recognition from others. They are examples of what biblical love is not: "Now a man named Ananias, together with his wife Sapphira, also sold a piece of property. With his wife's full knowledge he kept back part of the money for himself, but brought the rest and put it at the apostles' feet. Then Peter said, 'Ananias, how is it that Satan has so filled your heart that you have lied to the Holy Spirit and have kept for yourself some of the money you received for the land?'" (Acts 5:1-3). If Ananias and Sapphira were alive today, most pastors would parade them around the church as models of love and compassion. They would probably be promoted as leaders over the finance ministry! Yet when the apostle Peter confronted Ananias and Sapphira on their false pretenses, selfish motivations, and lying to the Holy Spirit, they both fell down at his feet and died.

Agape vs. Self-Seeking Love

Love in action is not love based on feelings. Paul assures us that "Love is patient, love is kind. It does not envy, it does not boast, it is not

THE UTOPIA OF A STRANGE LOVE

proud." Love also "does not dishonor others, it is not self-seeking, it is not easily angered, it keeps no record of wrongs. Love does not delight in evil but rejoices with the truth" (1 Cor. 13:4-6). When Paul says love is not self-seeking, he gives us a clear distinction between agape and self-centered loved. Self-love is the root of all selfishness and worldliness; it belongs to those who desire their own way to the exclusion of all others. Selfishness seeks the things that belong to oneself, one's own pleasure, profit, honor, and so on. In fact, the love of self is one of the conditions Paul describes as evidence of apostasy developing in the Last Days: "People will be lovers of themselves, lovers of money, boastful, proud, abusive, disobedient to their parents, ungrateful, unholy" (2 Tim. 3:2). Genuine biblical love—is always doing that which is best from the perspective of eternity, regardless of the consequences.

Paul describes the four strengths of love: Love "always protects, always trusts, always hopes, always perseveres" (1 Cor. 13:7). And love is permanent: "Love never fails. But where there are prophecies, they will cease; where there are tongues, they will be stilled; where there is knowledge, it will pass away. For we know in part and we prophesy in part, but when completeness comes, what is in part disappears" (1 Cor. 13:8-10). Agape love will last and remain unchanged indefinitely. Even the gifts of the Spirit, which the Corinthian Christians so esteemed and exalted, will fade away in eternity. But love will continue. Love is the greatest of the virtues because of its eternal state. "And now these three remain: faith, hope and love. But the greatest of these is love" (1 Cor. 13:13). Faith and hope will be fulfilled when we see Christ face-to-face, but love will endure forever.

How is it then that some conclude love is supreme based on these verses? We can hear things from others for so long that we just take them at face value until we search the scriptures ourselves. G. Campbell Morgan said that "examining this chapter [1 Corinthians 13] is like dissecting a flower to understand it. If you tear it apart too much, you lose the beauty." Sadly, the "love chapter" has not only been ripped apart but rewritten in our times. In the final analysis, what Paul is saying in the chapter is that love is the greater virtue, and it should be the primary motivation behind spiritual gifts operating within the church. He is not telling the church to choose between love and the other gifts. Rather, he is emphasizing that love is the focus, not any particular spiritual gift being exalted.

IS LOVE THE GREATEST?

Something else is critical to our understanding of love in a biblical context. Paul says, "Love does not delight in evil but rejoices with the truth" (1 Cor. 13:6). Love is not authentic if it excludes the truth. Without truth, love can be made to fit anyone's objective. Love can overlook the faults of others, but it cannot overlook the truth. Love is devoted to the truth, and it will never divorce the truth and marry a lie. Therefore, if love rejoices in the truth, how will it respond to error? Love confronts error and never compromises with it. True love does not remain quiet while error runs rampant destroying souls.

When writing to Titus, who was called to set the churches in order by establishing biblical leadership ("The reason I left you in Crete was that you might put in order what was left unfinished and appoint elders in every town, as I directed you"—Titus 1:5), Paul knew that in order for this to be accomplished, false teachers would need to be confronted and rendered inoperable. The reason he gave was this: "There are many rebellious people, full of meaningless talk and deception, especially those of the circumcision group. They must be silenced, because they are disrupting whole households by teaching things they ought not to teach—and that for the sake of dishonest gain" (Titus 1:10-11).

The silence coming from Christians today regarding unscriptural teaching on love is deafening! J. C. Ryle once said, "To regularly hear unscriptural teaching is a serious thing. It is a continual dropping of slow poison into the mind."[74] The enemy has convinced us that speaking out against and labeling some leaders as false is not showing the love of God. Holocaust survivor and Nobel Laureate Elie Wiesel said, "What hurts the victim most is not the cruelty of the oppressor, but the silence of the bystander."[75] Too many Christians believe calling untruthful teachers out will have a deleterious effect on unbelievers coming to Christ. I don't believe Jesus felt this way when He pronounced eight woes on the unscrupulous teachers of the law and the Pharisees in front of the crowd in the Gospel of Matthew. When questionable leaders go unchecked, we are giving them visual platforms in the church from which they can do irreparable damage. When followers of the Lord give tacit approval to such leaders, "many will follow their depraved conduct and will bring the way of truth into disrepute" (2 Pet. 2:2).

---

74. J. C. Ryle, *Warnings to the Churches* (Edinburgh: Banner of Truth, 1967).
75. Elie Wiesel, *Night* (New York City: Hill & Wang, 2006).

THE UTOPIA OF A STRANGE LOVE

The world is pleased to mock and slander the gospel of Jesus while watching false teachers negatively influence the church. Satan's plan is to prevent lost souls from being saved, and this is accomplished very effectively through ungodly leadership in the church. Thrown in with the bargain is the formidable damage done to the souls of those in the church by the same false leadership. This is what a false view of love has created.

The Silence of the Church

Silence is not a badge of honor and humility. When Adolf Hitler came to power in Germany, he scornfully dismissed the church and its leaders as an irrelevant voice posing no threat to his agenda. Sadly, Hitler was right. Many of the German churches remained quiet and looked the other way. Hitler said, "We should destroy the preachers by their notorious greed and self-indulgence. We shall thus be able to settle everything with them in perfect peace and harmony. I shall give them a few years reprieve, why should we quarrel? . . . They will betray their God for us, they will betray anything for the sake of their miserable jobs and income."[76] The church looked away, thinking that not confronting the evil and instead showing "love" would turn the tide. But this not only encouraged the sin, it directly strengthened the hands of the evildoers. Few voices were raised against the monstrous Nazi evil during that time. One of the few was Dietrich Bonhoeffer. He understood that love for Christ and others required courage to speak the truth even in unfavorable times. Bonhoeffer was deeply troubled by the church's silence:

> We the church must confess that we have not proclaimed often or clearly enough the message of the One God who has revealed Himself for all time in Christ Jesus, and who will tolerate no other gods beside Himself. She must confess her timidity, her cowardice, her evasiveness and her dangerous concessions. She was silent when she should have cried out because the blood of the innocent was crying aloud to heaven. . . . The church is guilty of the deaths of the weakest and most defenseless brothers of Jesus Christ. The church

---

76. Quoted in Laurence White, "The Sin of Silence: A message to American pastors and their congregations," September 6, 2000.

must confess that she has desired security and peace, quiet, possession, and honor to which she has no right. She has not born witness to the truth of God and by her silence, she has rendered herself guilty, because of her unwillingness to suffer for what she knows to be right.[77]

In its thunderous silence, the church became a traitor to the lordship of Christ. She failed to heed Bonhoeffer's prophetic words, and within a few years, Hitler's agenda was accomplished—with over eleven million people being murdered, including Dietrich Bonhoeffer himself. True biblical love never turns a blind eye to deception, error, and sin. The attitude that we should ignore these things and "just let God deal with it" is anything but biblical. Compromising for the sake of peace, acceptance, and approval is never the answer for devoted Christians.

This type of mindset draws minimal opposition from the enemy. Satan knows people have the ability to reassess their spiritual condition, so his plan is to keep them as comfortable as possible. It could even appear God is rewarding them because of their increased earthly achievements, adding credibility to the notion God is blessing them despite their unbiblical view of love. It is a view of love that compromises for the sake of adulation and approval.

What happened among the German churches happened first to the church at Corinth. In 1 Corinthians 5, we see a church that has become seduced by a false notion of grace and love. There was a particular man who was having a sexual relationship with his stepmother. This illicit relationship bore the same stigma as if the man had been having a sexual relationship with his own mother. Incestuous affairs were of course forbidden by the scriptures: "Do not have sexual relations with your father's wife; that would dishonor your father," intoned Leviticus 18:8. "A man is not to marry his father's wife; he must not dishonor his father's bed," said Deuteronomy 22:30.

This incestuous affair was even considered taboo by the pagan city of Corinth. To say that the city did not approve this sort of thing speaks volumes. Corinth was known as the hotbed of immorality. Living a blatant, licentious lifestyle was standard. The city had temple priestesses who served as prostitutes where men would go in and have sexual relations as part of their temple worship. The prostitutes would leave the temple to come into

---

77. Dietrich Bonhoeffer, *Ethics* (New York: Touchstone, 1995), 117.

THE UTOPIA OF A STRANGE LOVE

the city and sell their services in the marketplace. They lived the immoral life to the fullest, and the church allowed this to go on. The world was looking at the church and saying, "Even we know that is wrong!" That is what troubled the apostle Paul.

What outraged Paul the most was not just the man's sin but the Corinthian church's response to his sexual immorality. He asked, "And you are proud! Shouldn't you rather have gone into mourning and have put out of your fellowship the man who has been doing this?" (1 Cor. 5:2). There are perhaps two main reasons why the church looked the other way when it came to egregious sin. First, they rejected the authority of the Word of God. They overlooked the sin even after Paul said, "I wrote to you in my letter not to associate with sexually immoral people" (1 Cor. 5:9). Second, the church had a false view of love, which led directly to the rejection of scripture. With the rejection of scripture came a casual attitude toward sin.

What the church of Corinth displayed in this salacious situation was definitely not biblical love but rather the character traits of worldly love and undiscerning tolerance. Embracing tolerance just because it is politically correct will cause us to ignore what the scripture says about a particular issue so we can come across as more loving and accepting. But according to Paul, when the church remains silent, this is not evidence of walking in love but in pride. "Your boasting is not good. Don't you know that a little yeast leavens the whole batch of dough?" (1 Cor. 5:6). The Corinthians should have been grieving over the sin within their ranks, but they allowed sin to influence and corrupt the church at large.

How is it that when non-Christians divorce, due to adultery, we call them sinners? But when our favorite church leaders do the same, we call them human, under grace, and we allow them to hold on to leadership positions? We judge the person in the world, but we protect the one in the church. When someone in the church speaks against our personal idols, whether it is a sinning leader, smoking, drinking, or sexual perversion, it is common to hear, "Who are you to judge?" "That is not the love of God," "That is not your business," or "Just pray about it." According to Paul, this should never be. "What business is it of mine to judge those outside the church? Are you not to judge those inside? God will judge those outside. Expel the wicked person from among you" (1 Cor. 5:12-13).

When the love of God is mishandled and becomes something foreign to God's Word, we move from an apostolic view of love to a therapeutic view of love. When things are done contrary to God's Word, and we are not bothered by it, that is a good indicator we have attached ourselves to a strange love. This love is toxic, the mixture of poison and some truth. Biblical love is indeed the greater virtue, but without the complete truth, it loses its potency.

Love Is a Virtue, But Truth Is an Essential

I live in South Florida, which is home to many beautiful beaches. One day while performing baptisms at the beach, I began pondering the idea why biblical love could not exist apart from truth. Immediately, it hit me. The ocean is like love. The seashore/beach is like truth. The ocean is beautiful to behold and can bring times of enjoyment and times of refreshment. The seashore protects, guides, and places a boundary from destruction. If there were no seashore to govern the ocean, it could become a great catastrophe. If truth does not set the boundary on love, then love can turn from being something beautiful to something monstrous. In declaring how His people should fear Him, God speaks about how He created the seashore, in his providential act, to prevent flooding: "'Should you not fear me?' declares the Lord. 'Should you not tremble in my presence? I made the sand a boundary for the sea, an everlasting barrier it cannot cross. The waves may roll, but they cannot prevail; they may roar, but they cannot cross it'" (Jer. 5:22). As God has established the shorelines to restrain the mighty oceans, so has He ordained truth to restrain love. Love is a virtue, but truth is an essential. Truth is what gives love its meaning and value. If you remove the truth from love, you no longer have true love.

The apostle John spoke frequently in his Epistles about love. John was "the disciple whom Jesus loved" (John 13:23). He wrote often about our love for Christ and our love for one another, yet John never exalts love above truth. This fact is exhibited in his second (as well as his third) Epistle:

> The elder, To the lady chosen by God and to her children, whom I love in the truth—and not I only, but also all who know the truth—because of the truth, which lives in us and will be with us forever: Grace, mercy and peace from God the Father and from Jesus Christ, the Father's Son, will be with us in truth and love. It has given me great joy to find some of your children walking in the truth, just as the Father

THE UTOPIA OF A STRANGE LOVE

commanded us. And now, dear lady, I am not writing you a new command but one we have had from the beginning. I ask that we love one another. And this is love: that we walk in obedience to his commands. As you have heard from the beginning, his command is that you walk in love. (2 John 1-6)

John addresses himself as "the elder." At the time, John was the only apostle still living, and church history tells us he was the only apostle who did not die from martyrdom. The term *elder* speaks not only to John's advanced age but it speaks to his personal eyewitness testimony to the life of Jesus, His teachings, and His spiritual authority over the congregations. In the verses quoted above, John's use of love is always measured by what is true—"because of the truth, which lives in us and will be with us forever."

The common ground binding believers together is the truth of God's Word, explained in context, in order to produce sound living. Like the Word, truth never changes. If "truth" could be altered to fit the current taste, then it would not be biblical truth. Truth will always be absolute, and it will never be held captive by personal opinion. The glue holding believers together throughout the ages has been the truth of scripture. The necessity of truth and love is stated in 2 John 3: "Grace, mercy and peace from God the Father and from Jesus Christ, the Father's Son, will be with us in truth and love." Living out the truth develops a truly loving life. In the opening four verses of 2 John, the need for truth is stressed five times. This is no coincidence. Truth has always demanded repetition because of humankind's tendency to believe reformatted lies.

We learn by repetition. Once we learn our ABCs and the simple arithmetic that 2 + 2 = 4, we will not forget. Truth and love are the same way. Truth is the necessary essential for love to function properly. The apostle John writes to the lady, "It has given me great joy to find some of your children walking in the truth, just as the Father commanded us." In 3 John 4, the apostle repeats this sentiment: "I have no greater joy than to hear that my children are walking in the truth." John could have said he found great joy in seeing Christians practicing love. But he understood that if believers are walking in the truth of God's revelation, true love will be clearly visible in their lives. John intended believers to practice the kind of love that was in harmony with biblical truths of the faith.

How Is Love Demonstrated?

When love is in operation, it doesn't always have to be spoken—but it always has to be demonstrated. How is it demonstrated?

Love is demonstrated when it speaks the truth:

> So Christ himself gave the apostles, the prophets, the evangelists, the pastors and teachers, to equip his people for works of service, so that the body of Christ may be built up until we all reach unity in the faith and in the knowledge of the Son of God and become mature, attaining to the whole measure of the fullness of Christ. Then we will no longer be infants, tossed back and forth by the waves, and blown here and there by every wind of teaching and by the cunning and craftiness of people in their deceitful scheming. Instead, speaking the truth in love, we will grow to become in every respect the mature body of him who is the head, that is, Christ. From him the whole body, joined and held by every supporting ligament, grows and builds itself up in love, as each part does its work. (Eph. 4:11-16)

Love is demonstrated when it obeys the truth:

> If you love me, keep my commands. And I will ask the Father, and he will give you another advocate to help you and be with you forever—the Spirit of truth. The world cannot accept him, because it neither sees him nor knows him. But you know him, for he lives with you and will be in you. I will not leave you as orphans; I will come to you. Before long, the world will not see me anymore, but you will see me. Because I live, you also will live. On that day you will realize that I am in my Father, and you are in me, and I am in you. Whoever has my commands and keeps them is the one who loves me. The one who loves me will be loved by my Father, and I too will love them and show myself to them." (John 14:15-21)

Love is demonstrated when it feeds and protects:

THE UTOPIA OF A STRANGE LOVE

> When they had finished eating, Jesus said to Simon Peter, "Simon son of John, do you love me more than these?" "Yes, Lord," he said, "you know that I love you." Jesus said, "Feed my lambs." Again Jesus said, "Simon son of John, do you love me?" He answered, "Yes, Lord, you know that I love you." Jesus said, "Take care of my sheep." The third time he said to him, "Simon son of John, do you love me?" Peter was hurt because Jesus asked him the third time, "Do you love me?" He said, "Lord, you know all things; you know that I love you." Jesus said, "Feed my sheep. Very truly I tell you, when you were younger you dressed yourself and went where you wanted; but when you are old you will stretch out your hands, and someone else will dress you and lead you where you do not want to go." Jesus said this to indicate the kind of death by which Peter would glorify God. Then he said to him, "Follow me!" (John 21: 15-19)

Love is demonstrated when it inconveniences itself for the sake of others:

> I am the good shepherd. The good shepherd lays down his life for the sheep. The hired hand is not the shepherd and does not own the sheep. So when he sees the wolf coming, he abandons the sheep and runs away. Then the wolf attacks the flock and scatters it. The man runs away because he is a hired hand and cares nothing for the sheep. I am the good shepherd; I know my sheep and my sheep know me—just as the Father knows me and I know the Father—and I lay down my life for the sheep. I have other sheep that are not of this sheep pen. I must bring them also. They too will listen to my voice, and there shall be one flock and one shepherd. (John 10:11-16)

Love is demonstrated when it corrects and confronts error:

As Jesus started on his way, a man ran up to him and fell on his knees before him. "Good teacher," he asked, "what must

IS LOVE THE GREATEST?

I do to inherit eternal life?" "Why do you call me good?" Jesus answered. "No one is good—except God alone. You know the commandments: 'You shall not murder, you shall not commit adultery, you shall not steal, you shall not give false testimony, you shall not defraud, honor your father and mother.'" "Teacher," he declared, "all these I have kept since I was a boy." Jesus looked at him and loved him. "One thing you lack," he said. "Go, sell everything you have and give to the poor, and you will have treasure in heaven. Then come, follow me." At this the man's face fell. He went away sad, because he had great wealth. (Mark 10:17-22)

Love is demonstrated when it supports the work of God and helps other believers:

Dear friend, you are faithful in what you are doing for the brothers and sisters, even though they are strangers to you. They have told the church about your love. Please send them on their way in a manner that honors God. It was for the sake of the Name that they went out, receiving no help from the pagans. We ought therefore to show hospitality to such people so that we may work together for the truth. (3 John 5-8)

Command those who are rich in this present world not to be arrogant nor to put their hope in wealth, which is so uncertain, but to put their hope in God, who richly provides us with everything for our enjoyment. Command them to do good, to be rich in good deeds, and to be generous and willing to share. In this way they will lay up treasure for themselves as a firm foundation for the coming age, so that they may take hold of the life that is truly life. (1 Tim. 6:17-19)

The apostle Paul demonstrates love in his farewell speech to the Ephesian elders. He does not mention the word *love* in that speech, but biblical love is certainly exhibited through his life and his ministry:

THE UTOPIA OF A STRANGE LOVE

From Miletus, Paul sent to Ephesus for the elders of the church. When they arrived, he said to them: "You know how I lived the whole time I was with you, from the first day I came into the province of Asia. I served the Lord with great humility and with tears and in the midst of severe testing by the plots of my Jewish opponents. You know that I have not hesitated to preach anything that would be helpful to you but have taught you publicly and from house to house. I have declared to both Jews and Greeks that they must turn to God in repentance and have faith in our Lord Jesus. And now, compelled by the Spirit, I am going to Jerusalem, not knowing what will happen to me there. I only know that in every city the Holy Spirit warns me that prison and hardships are facing me. However, I consider my life worth nothing to me; my only aim is to finish the race and complete the task the Lord Jesus has given me—the task of testifying to the good news of God's grace. Now I know that none of you among whom I have gone about preaching the kingdom will ever see me again. Therefore, I declare to you today that I am innocent of the blood of any of you. For I have not hesitated to proclaim to you the whole will of God." (Acts 20:17-27)

The goal and purpose of every leader in the body of Christ should be to serve the Lord with humility, to preach repentance and faith in Christ, to testify to the good news of God's grace, and to proclaim the whole will of God. This is what biblical love looks like when governed by the truth. Truth without love will produce legalism. Love without truth will create sentimentalism. And unity without sound doctrine is the earmark of cultism. True love cannot be displayed unless truth has defined it. Love does not bring deliverance; only truth can do that. Scripture does not say, "You shall know love, and love shall set you free." It says, "You will know the truth, and the truth will set you free" (John 8:32).

True freedom and liberty can only be achieved by surrendering to absolute truth. While waiting in jail for his execution, Paul writes this to Timothy:

IS LOVE THE GREATEST?

For the Spirit God gave us does not make us timid, but gives us power, love and self-discipline. So do not be ashamed of the testimony about our Lord or of me his prisoner. Rather, join with me in suffering for the gospel, by the power of God. He has saved us and called us to a holy life—not because of anything we have done but because of his own purpose and grace. This grace was given us in Christ Jesus before the beginning of time, but it has now been revealed through the appearing of our Savior, Christ Jesus, who has destroyed death and has brought life and immortality to light through the gospel. And of this gospel I was appointed a herald and an apostle and a teacher. That is why I am suffering as I am. Yet this is no cause for shame, because I know whom I have believed, and am convinced that he is able to guard what I have entrusted to him until that day. (2 Tim. 1:7-12)

Love without the framework of biblical truth is dangerous. Propagating love to the exclusion of truth and sound doctrine has become Satan's wicked trick against God's end-time plan. In the hands of a generation that loves self more than anything, love without biblical truth will move countless souls to a highway that is not narrow but broad.

The Golden Calf of Relevance

How did the church of the living God get in the position of subverting the gospel with strange and damnable doctrines designed to tickle itching ears? How did we come to preach the love of God according to the dictates of the world? We were partakers of the redeeming power of Christ, and we were recipients of the mercy of God. We experienced the Red Sea moment when God made a way where there seemed to be no way. Yet, the very truths that freed us from sin and caused us to remain steadfast, including the truth that love is defined by biblical standards and not by the prevailing culture, are no longer accepted. Mathematician and theologian Blaise Pascal prophetically said, "Truth is so obscure in these times, and falsehood so established, that unless we love the truth, we cannot know it."[78] These words spoken by Pascal are still true today, even though he penned these words over three hundred fifty years ago. Sound doctrine is openly scorned as sinful and irrelevant. Scripture is no longer valued as infallible, sufficient, appropriate, and inerrant. In many churches, the Bible is used only as a reference point and not the authoritative source.

Expositional preaching, which details the content of the Bible as it appears in the text, is no longer the way most pastors preach today. We are living in the days in which scripture twisting is applauded, while true Bible teaching is considered boring and not anointed. The most popular style of teaching is usually topical and textual. Topical teaching is when one starts off with a topic and then searches for scripture texts to support the topic. Textual teaching uses a particular text to make a point but stops short of explaining what the text actually means in its context. What is commonly seen today, in both topical and textual preaching, the Bible is simply used to support a preacher's predetermined agenda. Discovering the true meaning of the verses—seeing things from God's point of view—is not the ultimate

---

78. Charles W. Eliot, *The Harvard Classics: Blaise Pascal Thoughts* (New York City: P. F. Collier & Son, 1963).

THE UTOPIA OF A STRANGE LOVE

goal. The ultimate goal is to prove the speaker's point. In other words, the most popular style of preaching today is where a preacher's opinion sits in authority over the scripture itself, which the Gospel of Mark says is letting go of the commands of God and holding on to human traditions.

> He replied, "Isaiah was right when he prophesied about you hypocrites; as it is written: 'These people honor me with their lips, but their hearts are far from me. They worship me in vain; their teachings are merely human rules.' You have let go of the commands of God and are holding on to human traditions." And he continued, "You have a fine way of setting aside the commands of God in order to observe your own traditions! For Moses said, 'Honor your father and mother,' and, 'Anyone who curses their father or mother is to be put to death.' But you say that if anyone declares that what might have been used to help their father or mother is Corban (that is, devoted to God)—then you no longer let them do anything for their father or mother. Thus you nullify the word of God by your tradition that you have handed down. And you do many things like that." (Mark 7:6-13)

How could those who once tasted God's good Word, and been enlightened by the Holy Spirit, turn away and believe another gospel, another spirit, and entertain another god? In the book of Exodus, there is a famous story of Israel's idolatry after being rescued from Egypt. The story begins by saying,

> When the people saw that Moses was so long in coming down from the mountain, they gathered around Aaron and said, "Come, make us gods who will go before us. As for this fellow Moses who brought us up out of Egypt, we don't know what has happened to him." Aaron answered them, "Take off the gold earrings that your wives, your sons and your daughters are wearing, and bring them to me." So all the people took off their earrings and brought them to Aaron. He took what they handed him and made it into an idol cast in the shape of a calf, fashioning it with a tool. Then

THE GOLDEN CALF OF RELEVANCE

> they said, "These are your gods, Israel, who brought you up out of Egypt." (Exod. 32:1-4)

The driving force behind Israel's worship was to have an idol of relevance. The perspective today has hardly changed. Everywhere one turns the word *relevant* is used, including in the church. It is usually suggested that in order for the church to reach the world it has to become "relevant," to get with the times. This kind of attitude comes from people who are driven by what they see. It is the same perspective we read about with the children of Israel, who after Moses delayed became impatient in their actions. They said, "Come, make us gods who will go before us. As for this fellow Moses who brought us up out of Egypt, we don't know what has happened to him." They were a generation that listened with their eyes.

We Listen with Our Eyes

We, too, are a generation that listens with our eyes. The return of Jesus seems delayed, so we think we have to alter His plan. In his second Epistle, Peter prophetically spoke about how scoffers will come in the Last Days, mocking the return of Christ:

> Dear friends, this is now my second letter to you. I have written both of them as reminders to stimulate you to wholesome thinking. I want you to recall the words spoken in the past by the holy prophets and the command given by our Lord and Savior through your apostles. Above all, you must understand that in the last days scoffers will come, scoffing and following their own evil desires. They will say, "Where is this 'coming' he promised? Ever since our ancestors died, everything goes on as it has since the beginning of creation." But they deliberately forget that long ago by God's word the heavens came into being and the earth was formed out of water and by water. By these waters also the world of that time was deluged and destroyed. By the same word the present heavens and earth are reserved for fire, being kept for the day of judgment and destruction of the ungodly. (2 Pet. 3:1-7)

THE UTOPIA OF A STRANGE LOVE

When most people read, "in the last days scoffers will come, scoffing and following their own evil desires," they tend to think the mockers will be those from the world. But this verse is talking about leaders from within the church who ridicule the coming of Jesus in order to fulfill their self-indulgent lifestyles. An example of this is one popular leader who is a part of the diabolical Word of Faith Movement, which teaches that one attains health and wealth through positive confession. He once told the audience, "Quit trying to escape out of this world. Stop with all of this 'I'm-ready-for-Jesus-to-come-back' talk. Jesus cannot come back until you get all of your stuff. I don't need my stuff in heaven, I need it now on earth." Instead of the crowd standing up and exiting the building, they stood up and celebrated.

When we become impatient, we become creative, viewing things out of the lens of the culture and self, rather than waiting on God to reveal His full counsel. This has been Satan's plan of deception against humanity since Adam and Eve in the Garden of Eden. After Satan influenced Eve's mind concerning her eyes being open in Genesis 3:4-5 ("You will not certainly die. . . . For God knows that when you eat from it your eyes will be opened, and you will be like God, knowing good and evil"), the Bible says, "When the woman saw that the fruit of the tree was good for food and pleasing to the eye, and also desirable for gaining wisdom, she took some and ate it. She also gave some to her husband, who was with her, and he ate it" (Gen. 3:6). There is no doubt Eve saw this particular tree very often. But after Satan speaks to her mind, the very tree she saw so regularly now appears desirable in a way it did not before.

How Deceiving Spirits Operate

Deceiving spirits operate by first working on the mind, the thought process, to move one to see things from another viewpoint—a viewpoint contrary to God's original purpose. Paul wrote to the Galatians,

> I am astonished that you are so quickly deserting the one who called you to live in the grace of Christ and are turning to a different gospel—which is really no gospel at all. Evidently some people are throwing you into confusion and are trying to pervert the gospel of Christ. But even if we or an angel from heaven should preach a gospel other than the one we preached to you, let them be under God's curse! As we have

already said, so now I say again: If anybody is preaching to you a gospel other than what you accepted, let them be under God's curse! (Gal. 1:6-9)

This was the very thing that led to the downfall of Lot's life. Listening with his eyes led Lot to a city that was eventually to experience the judgment of God. The Bible says,

> Lot looked around and saw that the whole plain of the Jordan toward Zoar was well watered, like the garden of the Lord, like the land of Egypt. (This was before the Lord destroyed Sodom and Gomorrah.) So Lot chose for himself the whole plain of the Jordan and set out toward the east. The two men parted company: Abram lived in the land of Canaan, while Lot lived among the cities of the plain and pitched his tents near Sodom. Now the people of Sodom were wicked and were sinning greatly against the Lord. (Gen. 13:10-13)

Lot represents the carnality of worldly believers who allow their eyes to determine God's will. There is great danger when we listen with our eyes. Lot knew the will of God concerning the promised land, but it did not look desirable to him. His eyes led him out of God's will and moved him into an area that appeared lovely but ultimately brought about a sad outcome. Lot even had the first option on where to go. "So Abram said to Lot, 'Let's not have any quarreling between you and me, or between your herders and mine, for we are close relatives. Is not the whole land before you? Let's part company. If you go to the left, I'll go to the right; if you go to the right, I'll go to the left'" (Gen. 13:8-9). Lot's decision to move out of God's will led him into compromise and tolerance. He pitched his tent near Sodom because the land of Jordan appeared to offer him something his current place seemed to be lacking. This is the driving force behind the "relevant" talk and what led the children of Israel to desire another god. They went to Aaron and demanded he make them a god to lead them.

Unbiblical leadership is to blame for many aberrations within the church today. Yet we have to realize that there is so much unbiblical leadership because there is a market for it. The problem was not just with Aaron but also with the people who cried, "Come, make us gods who will

THE UTOPIA OF A STRANGE LOVE

go before us." Nor did the problem begin with King Saul, but rather with the people's demand for a king, when God was supposed to be their King:

> When Samuel grew old, he appointed his sons as Israel's leaders. The name of his firstborn was Joel and the name of his second was Abijah, and they served at Beersheba. But his sons did not follow his ways. They turned aside after dishonest gain and accepted bribes and perverted justice. So all the elders of Israel gathered together and came to Samuel at Ramah. They said to him, "You are old, and your sons do not follow your ways; now appoint a king to lead us, such as all the other nations have." But when they said, "Give us a king to lead us," this displeased Samuel; so he prayed to the Lord. And the Lord told him: "Listen to all that the people are saying to you; it is not you they have rejected, but they have rejected me as their king. As they have done from the day I brought them up out of Egypt until this day, forsaking me and serving other gods, so they are doing to you. Now listen to them; but warn them solemnly and let them know what the king who will reign over them will claim as his rights." Samuel told all the words of the Lord to the people who were asking him for a king. He said, "This is what the king who will reign over you will claim as his rights: He will take your sons and make them serve with his chariots and horses, and they will run in front of his chariots. Some he will assign to be commanders of thousands and commanders of fifties, and others to plow his ground and reap his harvest, and still others to make weapons of war and equipment for his chariots. He will take your daughters to be perfumers and cooks and bakers. He will take the best of your fields and vineyards and olive groves and give them to his attendants. He will take a tenth of your grain and of your vintage and give it to his officials and attendants. Your male and female servants and the best of your cattle and donkeys he will take for his own use. He will take a tenth of your flocks, and you yourselves will become his slaves. When that day comes, you will cry out for relief from the king you have

chosen, but the Lord will not answer you in that day." (1 Sam. 8:1-18)

Israel's leaders wanted a king, "such as all the other nations have." This would make them relevant. The objective of being relevant is to meet the expectations of the people. It is pure humanism to feel the need to be relevant to the culture while turning our backs on God. Humanism puts our desires, our needs, and our wills at the center of God's plan. This is what happens in the time of apostasy. The will of the people is exalted above God's will, allowing error to set in while people shift away from God's original intentions. In the Old Testament, God raised up prophets to bring His people back to Him. Prophetic voices indicated His covenant people had departed from His ways and oracles. "This is what the Lord says: 'Stand at the crossroads and look; ask for the ancient paths, ask where the good way is, and walk in it, and you will find rest for your souls.' But you said, 'We will not walk in it.' I appointed watchmen over you and said, 'Listen to the sound of the trumpet!' But you said, 'We will not listen'" (Jer. 6:16-17).

A true word from God will confront the present condition in order to move people back to Him. We see this all throughout the scriptures in the ministry of a prophet. Jesus, the Prophet, is operating in this same pattern in His messages to the churches in Revelation. Laodicea was one particular church that humanism had captured.

Laodiceanism

To the angel of the church in Laodicea write: These are the words of the Amen, the faithful and true witness, the ruler of God's creation. I know your deeds, that you are neither cold nor hot. I wish you were either one or the other! So, because you are lukewarm—neither hot nor cold—I am about to spit you out of my mouth. You say, 'I am rich; I have acquired wealth and do not need a thing.' But you do not realize that you are wretched, pitiful, poor, blind and naked. I counsel you to buy from me gold refined in the fire, so you can become rich; and white clothes to wear, so you can cover your shameful nakedness; and salve to put on your eyes, so you can see. Those whom I love I rebuke and

THE UTOPIA OF A STRANGE LOVE

discipline. So be earnest and repent. Here I am! I stand at the door and knock. If anyone hears my voice and opens the door, I will come in and eat with that person, and they with me. To the one who is victorious, I will give the right to sit with me on my throne, just as I was victorious and sat down with my Father on his throne. Whoever has ears, let them hear what the Spirit says to the churches. (Rev. 3:14-22)

Many interpreters believe the seven churches of Revelation 2–3 represent seven different church ages—starting with the time of the apostles and ending with the church that will be represented in the end times. If that is indeed the case, then the church in Laodicea would represent a large percentage of today's church. Whether that view is correct or not, there are overwhelming similarities with the church at Laodicea and the majority of what we see today. It is important to examine these texts closely to pull out the true meaning of what Christ is saying to this church.

To understand this matter in detail, we must understand that there is a common pattern shared in all the letters to the seven churches. Each letter is, first, Christ's description of Himself; second, Christ's evaluation of the church's condition, beginning with the words *I know*; third, the Lord's words of comfort and correction based on His assessment of the church; fourth, Jesus' command that everyone "listen to what the Spirit says to the churches"; and fifth, Christ's promised blessings to those who overcome. There was one thing, however, that separated the church in Laodicea from the others: the Laodicean church was the only church about which Christ had nothing good to say. Christ, who is the essence of love, absolutely finds nothing to His liking in this church. Actually, their self-deception sickened Him: "'I am rich; I have acquired wealth and do not need a thing.' But you do not realize that you are wretched, pitiful, poor, blind and naked" (Rev. 3:17). Many today would be shocked by these negative words.

Laodicea's Greek name is an indicator of the church's behavior. As with many Greek names, it reveals something about its character. The name comes from two Greek words, *Lao*—meaning the people, and *Dictaomi*—meaning opinions, decisions, and judgments. Laodicea refers to the governing or ruling opinions of people. In the case of the Laodicean church, the people's ideas were ruling in place of God's ideas. The church operated according to men's ways, to the exclusion of God's way. When the Lord described Himself with, "These are the words of the Amen, the faithful and

THE GOLDEN CALF OF RELEVANCE

true witness, the ruler of God's creation" (Rev. 3:14), this revealed what He thought about their self-governing. In the words of New Testament scholar Richard Mayhue, "Christ comes to the leadership of the church as an Accuser, not their Advocate."[79] And this is the testimony of every true prophet of God; they are God's loyal soldiers, but the task they are given makes them seem like turncoats.

What qualifies Jesus to deliver this indictment in Revelation 3:17? The assessment that the Laodicean church was wretched, pitiful, poor, blind, and naked is coming from the One who is eternal and who ought to know. First, "these are the words of the Amen" (Rev. 3:14). The *Amen* signifies certainty and affirms something true. Jesus Christ is the ultimate source of truth; He alone has the last word on what is and what is not true. He alone is the Guarantor of all God's promises. The second qualification is that Jesus is "the faithful and true witness." He is faithful because His words are completely trustworthy, and He is true because it is impossible for His witness to be wrong. He is perfect and accurate in His witness. Third, He address Himself as "the ruler of God's creation." Some New Testament translations use the phrase, "Beginning of the creation of God." This does not mean Jesus was the first being God created. That belief is commonly taught in false religions, such as the Jehovah's Witnesses. Being the beginning of creation means Jesus was the "firstborn of creation"—that is, He is the ruler or originator over all creation. He is the Alpha and the Omega. All things begin with Him, and all things will end with Him. "Through him all things were made; without him nothing was made that has been made" (John 1:3).

Jesus Christ is the ultimate source of truth. And because He is the source of truth, all that He has eyewitnessed is free from any error. His diagnosis of the church's ills is perfectly accurate. These things are true because He is the Ruler, the Owner of the church, the only one qualified to render this indictment without rebuttal from those He created. Jesus states who He is to prevent any idea of a church led and self-governed by their own opinion. As for Laodicea, which as I have mentioned, means the governing or ruling opinions of people rather than God, the Lord measured them and found them neither hot nor cold, but lukewarm: "I know your deeds, that you are neither cold nor hot. I wish you were either one or the

---

79. Richard Mayhue, *What Would Jesus Say About Your Church?* (Scotland: Christian Focus, 1995).

THE UTOPIA OF A STRANGE LOVE

other! So, because you are lukewarm—neither hot nor cold—I am about to spit you out of my mouth" (Rev. 3:15-16).

Too many people have misinterpreted the meaning of hot and cold. It is commonly thought that *hot* means saved, while *cold* means unsaved. But that is not correct. *Hot* means zeal, the zeal that produces spiritual healing. *Cold* means refreshing. Jesus was using the water conditions in Laodicea to illustrate His message. Laodicea did not have their own source of water, so they depended on water to flow from two nearby cities, Hierapolis and Colossae. Hierapolis was known for their hot springs, which were used for medicinal purposes, whereas Colossae was known for their extremely refreshing cold water that flowed down from the mountains. By the time the water reached Laodicea from these two cities, it was lukewarm. What Jesus was saying to this church was, "I wish you were hot to bring healing to those who are sick, or cold to bring refreshment to those who are weary, but you are neither."

Lukewarmness is a picture of compromise, deception, and admixture. It is what happens when we play the middle, when our desire is to become relevant to a culture forever changing. It is also what happens when the church alters the message of the Cross and abandons hard truths for the sake of being well liked. Some go to great lengths to make sure their messages run in agreement with the culture—and this is the fruit of spiritual idolatry. In essence, spiritual idolatry is when people begin exalting their will above God's. It is man's attempt to use God, only to serve man's desires or wishes. We see this in King Saul's life, after God tells him to completely destroy the wicked Amalekites, but he alters the command in order to keep the best for himself and the people:

> "I regret that I have made Saul king, because he has turned away from me and has not carried out my instructions." Samuel was angry, and he cried out to the Lord all that night. . . . And he sent you on a mission, saying, "Go and completely destroy those wicked people, the Amalekites; wage war against them until you have wiped them out." Why did you not obey the Lord? Why did you pounce on the plunder and do evil in the eyes of the Lord? "But I did obey the Lord," Saul said. "I went on the mission the Lord assigned me. I completely destroyed the Amalekites and brought back Agag their king. The soldiers took sheep

THE GOLDEN CALF OF RELEVANCE

and cattle from the plunder, the best of what was devoted to God, in order to sacrifice them to the Lord your God at Gilgal." But Samuel replied: "Does the Lord delight in burnt offerings and sacrifices as much as in obeying the Lord? To obey is better than sacrifice, and to heed is better than the fat of rams. For rebellion is like the sin of divination, and arrogance like the evil of idolatry. Because you have rejected the word of the Lord, he has rejected you as king." (1 Sam. 15:11; 18-23)

What the pagan cultures had in wooden statutes, we have in our hearts. And what we have in our hearts manifests in our life practices. Idolatry gives humankind a measure of religious and emotional gratification apart from the totality of God's Word. It is a religious substitution of the requirements of God. Once idolatry takes root in the heart, pride develops. This is why the voice of a prophet disturbs the masses; the prophet's message is in direct conflict with the pride and exalted will of the people. They always demand a choice—if God is not God, worship the idol and serve human interests; but if God is God, repent of idolatry and serve Him.

We see this played out in the Exodus story previously mentioned. Once again, here is the relevant text:

> When the people saw that Moses was so long in coming down from the mountain, they gathered around Aaron and said, "Come, make us gods who will go before us. As for this fellow Moses who brought us up out of Egypt, we don't know what has happened to him." Aaron answered them, "Take off the gold earrings that your wives, your sons and your daughters are wearing, and bring them to me." So all the people took off their earrings and brought them to Aaron. He took what they handed him and made it into an idol cast in the shape of a calf, fashioning it with a tool. Then they said, "These are your gods, Israel, who brought you up out of Egypt." (Exod. 32:1-4)

The Israelites were tired of waiting for Moses to return from the mountain, and they demanded Aaron to "make us gods who will go before us"—idols of relevance to worship, something they could see and

THE UTOPIA OF A STRANGE LOVE

handle, instead of relying on the living God. They wanted a god they could control, govern, and worship their own way. Keep in mind that this happened after God had already explicitly forbidden the creating and worshiping of graven images:

> You shall not make for yourself an image in the form of anything in heaven above or on the earth beneath or in the waters below. You shall not bow down to them or worship them; for I, the Lord your God, am a jealous God, punishing the children for the sin of the parents to the third and fourth generation of those who hate me. (Exod. 20:4-5)

Notice this idol was built from the resources of the people of Israel, consisting of the gold earrings worn by the wives, sons, and daughters. Aaron "took what they handed him and made it into an idol cast in the shape of a calf" (Exod. 32:4). People will sacrifice abundantly to finance their personal idols. It is interesting that Aaron not only asked for individual income—he asked for the income belonging to the entire family. From that time to this, countless families have lost their family inheritance and met their ruin by supporting and believing a lie. The resources of the people were *supposed* to be used to build God's tabernacle.

> The Lord said to Moses, "Tell the Israelites to bring me an offering. You are to receive the offering for me from everyone whose heart prompts them to give. These are the offerings you are to receive from them: gold, silver and bronze; blue, purple and scarlet yarn and fine linen; goat hair; ram skins dyed red and another type of durable leather; acacia wood; olive oil for the light; spices for the anointing oil and for the fragrant incense; and onyx stones and other gems to be mounted on the ephod and breastpiece." (Exod. 25:1-7)

Instead, Aaron and the children of Israel used the gold earrings to build something false. In our own day, Satan has convinced many people of God to take the resources God has given them to support fraudulent ministries. We support disingenuous prophets by applauding their sermons,

THE GOLDEN CALF OF RELEVANCE

attending their conferences, watching their television shows, purchasing their books, and buying their teaching materials. We send them offerings to aid and abet their spreading of unashamed lies across media outlets. We attend their churches and give money tirelessly, for supposed promises that never show up. In the case of one devious televangelist, we send money to allow him to buy the most expensive private jet available on the market. Untold numbers of souls are corrupted, and we have supported it. Wake up, people of God! The apostle of love told us that . . .

> Anyone who runs ahead and does not continue in the teaching of Christ does not have God; whoever continues in the teaching has both the Father and the Son. If anyone comes to you and does not bring this teaching, do not take them into your house or welcome them. Anyone who welcomes them shares in their wicked work. (2 John 9-11)

Satan will give us any type of god we want, in exchange for our money and our lives. How long are we going to continue following the false promises coming from televangelists? How long are we going to continue to strengthen the hands of evil-doers? If we would but read and believe all the warnings in the scriptures, the same as we do with all the promises of scripture, many wolves would starve to death—thereby sustaining the people of God. Instead, we feed them and let them grow and flourish.

When Aaron fashioned the idol into the shape of a calf, the people proclaimed, "These are your gods, Israel, who brought you up out of Egypt" (Exod. 32:4). They did not deny it was the true God who rescued them from bondage. Yet they exchanged who He really is into an idol they could personally control and relate to. In that way they could acknowledge the true God's power but form an image of Him to allow them to serve their sensual pleasures with no disapproval. The children of Israel verbally confessed God as their Savior yet reduced Him to a familiar image relative to their culture back in Egypt.

Aaron and the Israelites took their eyes off God, but God did not take His eyes off them. He saw and heard everything:

> Then the Lord said to Moses, "Go down, because your people, whom you brought up out of Egypt, have become corrupt. They have been quick to turn away from what I

commanded them and have made themselves an idol cast in the shape of a calf. They have bowed down to it and sacrificed to it and have said, 'These are your gods, Israel, who brought you up out of Egypt.' "I have seen these people," the Lord said to Moses, "and they are a stiff-necked people. Now leave me alone so that my anger may burn against them and that I may destroy them. Then I will make you into a great nation." (Exod. 32:7-10)

What made God so angry as to change His allegiance from "His" people to tell Moses that they are "your" people? God was angry at both the people's ungodly demand to "make us gods who will go before us" as well as the leadership of Aaron to meet the demand. When Aaron saw how happy the people were about the idol he had fashioned, "he built an altar in front of the calf and announced, 'Tomorrow there will be a festival to the Lord'" (Exod. 32:5). This ambition to be relevant to the culture produced what is now called *syncretism*. Syncretism is the attempt to assimilate differing or opposite doctrines and practices, especially between philosophical and religious systems, resulting in a new system altogether where the fundamental structure and tenets of each is changed.

Syncretism in Christianity occurs when the essential character of the faith is confused with elements from the culture. Chuck Colson said that "Syncretism occurs when ideas, practices, and entire worldviews are imported into a Christian frame of reference, so that Biblical terms are used to describe nonbiblical notions, and unbiblical points of view and practices are dressed up in the language of Christian faith."[80] He continued to say, "Syncretism is a challenge to the Church in every era. Syncretism refers to the practice of wedding false worldviews with the worldview of the Gospel, so that the truth of the Gospel is made captive to unbelieving agendas, and the followers of Christ are robbed of the power of the faith." This sort of incompatible mixture of worldviews is what plagued the church in Laodicea. The church needs to understand that God absolutely hates combining the gospel with anything else. He despises any additions and subtractions to the gospel message.

---

80. Chuck Colson with T. M. Moore, "Guard Against Syncretism," February 2014.

THE GOLDEN CALF OF RELEVANCE

Satan knows this very well, and that is why he uses syncretism to separate God from His people. God always has viewed syncretism as a threat to His people:

> The Lord your God will cut off before you the nations you are about to invade and dispossess. But when you have driven them out and settled in their land, and after they have been destroyed before you, be careful not to be ensnared by inquiring about their gods, saying, "How do these nations serve their gods? We will do the same." You must not worship the Lord your God in their way, because in worshiping their gods, they do all kinds of detestable things the Lord hates. They even burn their sons and daughters in the fire as sacrifices to their gods." (Deut. 12:29-31)

Dr. Harry Ironside said, "Truth mixed with error is equivalent to all error, except that it is more innocent looking and, therefore, more dangerous. God hates such a mixture!"[81] Truth is always the loser when it is

---

81. Harry Ironside (1876–1951), in his article titled, "Exposing Error: Is it Worthwhile?" from *The Projector* website, Dec. 1974. "Objection is often raised even by some sound in the faith—regarding the exposure of error as being entirely negative and of no real edification. Of late, the hue and cry has been against any and all negative teaching. But the brethren who assume this attitude forget that a large part of the New Testament, both of the teaching of our blessed Lord Himself and the writings of the apostles, is made up of this very character of ministry—namely, showing the Satanic origin and, therefore, the unsettling results of the propagation of erroneous systems which Peter, in his second Epistle, so definitely refers to as 'damnable heresies' (2 Pet. 2:1). Our Lord prophesied, 'Many false prophets shall rise, and shall deceive many' (Matt. 24:11). Within our own day, how many false prophets have risen; and oh, how many are the deceived! Paul predicted, 'I know this, that after my departing shall grievous wolves enter in among you, not sparing the flock. Also of your own selves shall men arise, speaking perverse things, to draw away disciples after them. Therefore watch' (Acts 20:29-31). My own observation is that these 'grievous wolves,' alone and in packs, are not sparing even the most favoured flocks. Under-shepherds in these 'perilous times' will do well to note the apostle's warning: 'Take heed therefore unto yourselves, and to all the flock, over the which the Holy Ghost hath made you overseers' (Acts 20:28). It is as important in these days as in Paul's—in fact, it is increasingly important—to expose the many types of false teaching that, on every hand, abound more and more. We are called upon to 'contend earnestly for the faith once for all delivered to the saints' (Jude 1:3), while we hold the truth in love. The faith means the whole body of revealed truth, and to contend for all of God's truth necessitates some

THE UTOPIA OF A STRANGE LOVE

compromised with error, for truth gives up everything, but error has nothing to give up. This is why God was moved with wrath when He saw the idol Aaron made, and it was the reason Christ was moved with disgust over the church in Laodicea. When syncretism is allowed in the church, and when it goes unchecked, the gospel is lost as the church simply conforms to what is already present in the culture. This is the end result of lukewarmness, the golden calf of relevance. Lukewarmness is the result of something defiled,

---

negative teaching. The choice is not left with us. Jude said he preferred a different, a pleasanter theme: 'Beloved, when I gave all diligence to write unto you of the common salvation, it was needful for me to write unto you, and exhort you that ye should earnestly contend for the faith which was once delivered unto the saints. For there are certain men crept in unawares, who were before of old ordained to this condemnation, ungodly men, turning the grace of our God into lasciviousness, and denying the only Lord God, and our Lord Jesus Christ' (Jude 3–4). Paul likewise admonishes us to 'have no fellowship with the unfruitful works of darkness, but rather reprove them' (Eph. 5:11). This does not imply harsh treatment of those entrapped by error—quite the opposite. If it be objected that exposure to error necessitates unkind reflection upon others who do not see as we do, our answer is: it has always been the duty of every loyal servant of Christ to warn against any teaching that would make Him less precious or cast reflection upon His finished redemptive work and the all-sufficiency of His present service as our great High Priest and Advocate. Every system of teaching can be judged by what it sets forth as to these fundamental truths of the faith. 'What think ye of Christ?' is still the true test of every creed. The Christ of the Bible is certainly not the Christ of any false '-ism.' Each of the cults has its hideous caricature of our lovely Lord. Let us who have been redeemed at the cost of His precious blood be 'good soldiers of Jesus Christ' (2 Tim. 2:3). As the battle against the forces of evil waxes ever more hot, we have need for God-given valour. There is constant temptation to compromise. 'Let us go forth therefore unto Him without the camp, bearing His reproach' (Heb. 13:13). It is always right to stand firmly for what God has revealed concerning His blessed Son's Person and work. The 'father of lies' deals in half-truths and specializes in most subtle fallacies concerning the Lord Jesus, our sole and sufficient Savior. Error is like leaven of which we read, 'A little leaven leaveneth the whole lump' (Gal. 5:9). Truth mixed with error is equivalent to all error, except that it is more innocent looking and, therefore, more dangerous. God hates such a mixture! Any error, or any truth-and-error mixture, calls for definite exposure and repudiation. To condone such is to be unfaithful to God and His Word and treacherous to imperiled souls for whom Christ died. Exposing error is most unpopular work. But from every true standpoint it is worthwhile work. To our Savior, it means that He receives from us, His blood-bought ones, the loyalty that is His due. To ourselves, if we consider 'the reproach of Christ greater riches than the treasures of Egypt' (Heb. 11:26), it ensures future reward, a thousand-fold. And to souls 'caught in the snare of the fowler' (Prov. 29:5)—how many of them God only knows—it may mean light and life, abundant and everlasting."

THE GOLDEN CALF OF RELEVANCE

polluted, distorted, and ruined. In essence, this is the product of spiritual idolatry.

A Lack of Discernment

Jesus' charge against the Laodicean church is that they are self-deceived. One of the highest forms of deception is self-deception, because when a person is in this state, true biblical discernment is lacking. Discernment is the process of making careful distinctions in our thinking about truth. It is the ability to decide between truth and error, right and wrong. Having biblical discernment is another way of saying having a biblical mindset—having a mind so renewed and conformed to the Word of God that it serves as a filter through which every thought passes. With biblical discernment, everything not lining up with the Word of God is rejected. This mindset shapes a biblical view that the world and the moral standard by which we evaluate ideas and make decisions ultimately judge between truth and untruth. A biblical mindset thinks antithetically, and not with emotional feelings. Scripture informs a biblical mindset, not opinion.

In a generation desiring only to be coached and not taught, there is a famine of discernment. Only sound unbending doctrine can produce discernment, but biblical discernment has taken a nose dive in our world due to a steady increase of biblical illiteracy. Mike Gendron, leader of Proclaiming the Gospel ministry, has said that "Tragically, we are living in a time when evangelicals are following popular personalities instead of Christ and His word. . . . Since the word of God is not being proclaimed faithfully from many pulpits, there is a lack of discernment in the pews. Since people are not hearing the truth, they cannot discern what is false."[82] This dilemma has caused the church to turn away from "offensive" truths found in the Bible in order to please a consumer-driven market. Sadly, many evangelical Christians, and many more Christians of the non-evangelical variety, have become so driven by viewing things out of the lens of the culture and self that they end up despising the eternal. Satan has cunningly convinced us to sell our birthright (truth) for false pretenses and temporary success.

Discernment is unpopular these days, and biblical discernment is almost unheard of in some circles. In the church, preaching on right and

---

82. Mike Gendron, "Proclaiming the Gospel Ministries," in a Christian News Network article, November 15, 2014.

wrong rubs people the wrong way. Away with absolutes; only proclaim issues that are subjective to one's experience or opinion. Discernment ministries are repeatedly reviled for being divisive and unloving. Yet Paul did not call discernment unloving. He called it love:

> And this is my prayer: that your love may abound more and more in knowledge and depth of insight, so that you may be able to discern what is best and may be pure and blameless for the day of Christ. (Phil. 1:9-10)

Paul tells the saints at Philippi he is praying that their love for one another would be based on discernment of what is best. True love is never blind, but it is perceptive and it is able to evaluate (judge) people and circumstances accurately.

Christ's problem with the church of Laodicea is that they are not even aware they are deceived! Spiritual blindness has caused them to misconceive their spiritual state: "You say, 'I am rich; I have acquired wealth and do not need a thing'" (Rev. 3:17). Notice Jesus' charge against them, which begins with, "You say." This term is in the present tense, meaning they were currently saying it. Christ is discerning their current attitude, not an attitude of the past. He is listening and watching their lives as they unfold now. The evaluation of their spiritual lives did not come from Jesus—it came from their own self-diagnosis and by measuring themselves with worldly standards.

The Disease of the Culture

In Laodicea as much as today, the disease of the culture has spread throughout the church. The world thinks we are successful by the accumulation of goods and power. What the church fails to see is that God's measuring tool of success is totally opposite of what the world approves. One can earn a promotion and still not have God. One can purchase a dream home and still not have God. One can obtain great wealth but still not have God. One can write a *New York Times* bestseller and not have God. Even the fastest growing and most popular church in the city is not guaranteed to have God. What spirit has convinced us that if something is new, or if some increase is involved, it is from God?

A LACK OF DISCERNMENT

The most dreadful thing imaginable is for a man or woman to die without knowing Jesus Christ as Lord and Savior of life. Yet they become wildly successful and comfortable, to the exclusion of God's will, and convince themselves they are in the will of God because they are successful and very rich. Seventeenth century English poet John Trapp once said, "To prosper in sin is the greatest tragedy that can befall a man this side of hell."[83]

Jesus responded to a man who wanted Him to get involved into a civil dispute:

> Jesus replied, "Man, who appointed me a judge or an arbitrator between you?" Then he said to them, "Watch out! Be on your guard against all kinds of greed; life does not consist in an abundance of possessions." (Luke 12:14-15)

God measures success by obedience—not by material substance! When God's purposes are accomplished, then success follows. It is often true that obeying God does not always produce earthly success. True faith does not always produce a desirable result because, in all honesty, obeying God can bring us into a life of great suffering, especially in times of gross apostasy.

Look at the life of Noah. Noah's obedience to God caused him go against the tide of the current culture. Scripture says, "By faith Noah, when warned about things not yet seen, in holy fear built an ark to save his family. By his faith he condemned the world and became heir of the righteousness that is in keeping with faith" (Heb. 11:7). K. P. Yohannan, the founder and international director of Gospel for Asia, says, "For Noah, preaching 120 years without results meant choosing the hard road year after year. . . . We cannot honestly, authentically, reasonably, and deliberately serve our Lord without the willingness to accept difficulties and inconveniences."[84]

Or look at the life of Moses. His obedience caused him to reject the riches and pleasures of Egypt and avoid the reproach of Christ:

> By faith Moses, when he had grown up, refused to be known as the son of Pharaoh's daughter. He chose to be mis-

---

83. Source unknown.
84. K. P. Yohannan in his 2009 article, "Which Road Will Travel On?"

> treated along with the people of God rather than to enjoy the fleeting pleasures of sin. He regarded disgrace for the sake of Christ as of greater value than the treasures of Egypt, because he was looking ahead to his reward. (Heb. 11:24-26)

The prophet Jeremiah's godly obedience caused him to face great persecution, and he received hate from his own people: "Alas, my mother, that you gave me birth, a man with whom the whole land strives and contends! I have neither lent nor borrowed, yet everyone curses me" (Jer. 15:10). Jeremiah's ministry covered over forty years, and for twenty-three of those years he preached the same message of repentance, false prophets, and judgment. If Jeremiah ministered today, I wonder how many would consider him a prophet sent by God—or an out of tune grumpy preacher sent by the enemy. How many would label him the weeping prophet? Or would they call him the critical and uncompassionate prophet? By our current standards for success in leadership, Jeremiah would clearly be considered a failure. After all, he had very few converts, and he preached a message that was out of touch with the culture. Besides this, he was financially poor, suffered greatly, prophesied judgment rather than personal blessings, and was hated by the masses. Jeremiah was not the person to invite to speak at the next church growth conference!

The Prophetic Message Is Eternal

Because they have a message that is eternal, true prophets are admired more after their death than they are in life. Time catches up with their message to validate whether or not they were truly sent from God. This happened in the life of A. W. Tozer. During Tozer's active speaking days, he preached himself right off the dais from many preaching circuits. To say the least, his messages were not always well received. Many of them were considered unloving, and they often focused on the topic of false leadership in the church. Tozer once said,

> Christianity is not changing but Christian leaders within Christianity are. They are too much in the ways of the world. . . . They have often adopted the patterns of the business world of Madison Avenue for ministry, and held the example of those holy ones who had gone on before in disdain. . . .

A LACK OF DISCERNMENT

> Pop-psychology has become more important than the plain teaching of the Bible. Tradition has become a bad word, and woe be to the minister who is referred to as "traditional.". . . It seems like Christianity is in the hands of those who desire to be more like the world than like Christ.[85]

Yet today, no matter the denominational affiliation, many are quoting Tozer, and he is one of the most widely-read devotional authors in the Christian world. We are blessed by his ministry, but the price he paid to obey God was a heavy expense.

Considering Laodicea again, the Lord now counters their opinion ("I am rich; I have acquired wealth and do not need a thing") with a heart-piercing assessment of their true spiritual condition: "You do not realize that you are wretched, pitiful, poor, blind and naked" (Rev. 3:17). This sort of preaching would certainly not be encouraged today.

Jesus Christ's love for His church does not cause Him to shrink back or alter His message so no one will be offended. True love does not pull punches, and it does not work flattery. Solomon wrote that "a lying tongue hates those it hurts, and a flattering mouth works ruin" (Prov. 26:28). Walking in biblical love is at times painful, but true love demands telling the truth regardless of the consequences. The Laodiceans believed they had acquired wealth and needed nothing, but Jesus tells them they do not even know their own state of affairs.

What Jesus says about the Laodiceans is more important than their view of themselves. Pragmatic minds fail to receive this type of truth because their blindness has caused them to overlook that they are really spiritually poor, unclothed, and wretched. Spiritual blindness is worse than physical blindness. Blind Bartimaeus was able to see in Jesus what the spiritual leaders could not:

> Then they came to Jericho. As Jesus and his disciples, together with a large crowd, were leaving the city, a blind man, Bartimaeus (which means "son of Timaeus"), was sitting by the roadside begging. When he heard that it was Jesus of Nazareth, he began to shout, "Jesus, Son of

---

85. A. W. Tozer, ed. James L. Snyder, *Reclaiming Christianity: A Call to Authentic Faith* (Minneapolis: BethanyHouse, 2009), 7–8.

David, have mercy on me!" Many rebuked him and told him to be quiet, but he shouted all the more, "Son of David, have mercy on me!" Jesus stopped and said, "Call him." So they called to the blind man, "Cheer up! On your feet! He's calling you." Throwing his cloak aside, he jumped to his feet and came to Jesus. "What do you want me to do for you?" Jesus asked him. The blind man said, "Rabbi, I want to see." "Go," said Jesus, "your faith has healed you." Immediately he received his sight and followed Jesus along the road. (Mark 10:46-52)

Even in the midst of painful truths, Christ offers the Laodiceans a remedy. He strongly advises them to buy counsel from Him and stop relying on their own misguided perceptions. True change starts with a word from God and an honest evaluation of ourselves. We need to examine ourselves by the scriptures to see if we are in the faith, as the apostle Paul warned: "Examine yourselves to see whether you are in the faith; test yourselves. Do you not realize that Christ Jesus is in you—unless, of course, you fail the test?" (2 Cor. 13:5).

Spiritual Blindness

According to Proverbs 18:1, "An unfriendly person pursues selfish ends and against all sound judgment starts quarrels." The unfriendly person referred to in this verse is antisocial, self-centered, conceited, lacking in discernment, and unreasonable. If we are going to pursue wisdom, knowledge, and grace, we have to want them. The apostle Paul told us to "eagerly desire the greater gifts" (1 Cor. 12:31). To do that, we must retire out of the noise of this world by diverting our attention from selfish and unsocial endeavors and by seeking an excellent sense of what is good and true. Spiritual "unfriendliness" is one form of spiritual blindness. To counter it we must surround ourselves with people who will hold us accountable, who are scripture-driven, who understand the ways of God, and who will be independent of our own expectations.

In spite of their self-deception and lack of discernment, Jesus offers repentance to the church in Laodicea:

> I counsel you to buy from me gold refined in the fire, so you can become rich; and white clothes to wear, so you can cover your shameful nakedness; and salve to put on your eyes, so you can see. Those whom I love I rebuke and discipline. So be earnest and repent. Here I am! I stand at the door and knock. If anyone hears my voice and opens the door, I will come in and eat with that person, and they with me. To the one who is victorious, I will give the right to sit with me on my throne, just as I was victorious and sat down with my Father on his throne. Whoever has ears, let them hear what the Spirit says to the churches. (Rev. 3:18-22)

The Amen councils the Laodiceans to buy "gold refined in the fire," which is a picture of true faith. He says they should wear white clothes to "cover your shameful nakedness," which is another way of saying they must put on biblical righteousness. Jesus also councils the Laodiceans to use "salve to put on your eyes, so you can see." The reference here is to spiritual sight, or discernment. All of these things outline the pursuit of true wisdom.

Christ's strong words of rebuke in the letter to the church in Laodicea is not an indicator of Him being "negative" or of Him having a "critical spirit"; rather, His rebuke shows His love. His love for this church shows His desire for the Laodiceans to repent and be restored back to their proper position. If Jesus' ultimate desire was for them to be judged, no warning would have been given. If the Lord did not love them, then it stands to reason He would simply ignore declaring any warning. But refusing to give a warning would be hate. The book of Proverbs tells us that "Whoever spares the rod hates their children, but the one who loves their children is careful to discipline them" (Prov. 13:24). God tells the prophet Ezekiel, "If righteous people turn away from their righteous behavior and ignore the obstacles I put in their way, they will die. And if you do not warn them, they will die in their sins. None of their righteous acts will be remembered, and I will hold you responsible for their deaths" (Ezek. 3:30).

Convincing and Rebuking

The Holy Spirit instructed Paul, who later instructs Timothy, his son in the faith, to preach the Word in season or out of season:

THE UTOPIA OF A STRANGE LOVE

> In the presence of God and of Christ Jesus, who will judge the living and the dead, and in view of his appearing and his kingdom, I give you this charge: Preach the word; be prepared in season and out of season; correct, rebuke and encourage—with great patience and careful instruction. (2 Tim. 4:1-2)

Of this text, John MacArthur says, "The faithful preacher must proclaim the Word when it's popular and/or convenient, and when it is not; when it seems suitable to do so, and when it seems not. The dictates of popular culture, tradition, reputation, acceptance, or esteem in the community (or in the church) must never alter the true preacher's commitment to proclaim God's Word."[86]

Convincing and rebuking is the negative side of preaching, and it is just as important as the positive side of preaching. When Moses returned from the mountains and saw the calf Aaron had fashioned, and the people dancing, his anger exploded:

> When Moses approached the camp and saw the calf and the dancing, his anger burned and he threw the tablets out of his hands, breaking them to pieces at the foot of the mountain. And he took the calf the people had made and burned it in the fire; then he ground it to powder, scattered it on the water and made the Israelites drink it. (Exod. 32:19-20)

Did Moses need a class in anger management? No, but his love for God and God's people required a strong reaction. One cannot sit idly while the Word of God is being abused and neglected. This moved Moses to righteous indignation, and it should move us as well. If not, it is time to check our love for God.

If anyone can see another god being worshipped instead of the God who has redeemed us, and not be bothered by it, that person is not walking in love. Perhaps they have embraced tolerance, but they are not walking in love. We show what little conviction we have when we embrace tolerance.

---

86. John MacArthur, *The MacArthur Study Bible* (Nashville: Thomas Nelson, 1997), 1880.

A LACK OF DISCERNMENT

Sometimes the only real conviction we have is against those who speak contrary to our personal desires.

The message Jesus preached is the message we desperately need today: repentance. Repentance is not simply a message about changing our mind; it is a message to turn from our sin, our compromise, and our delusional views. Repentance will always be on the heart of God when His people are in apostasy. When the church falls in love with the world and therefore becomes adulterers and enemies with God, the heart of God will be calling not for us to be relevant, to dream big visions, to maximize our potential, or to pursue our goals, but for us to return to our first love.

> You adulterous people, don't you know that friendship with the world means enmity against God? Therefore, anyone who chooses to be a friend of the world becomes an enemy of God. Or do you think Scripture says without reason that he jealously longs for the spirit he has caused to dwell in us? But he gives us more grace. That is why Scripture says: "God opposes the proud but shows favor to the humble." (James 4:4-6)

When Moses saw the idol, he didn't recite to the people how much God loved them and how God knew their hearts. Instead, he tore the idol down, confronted the sin, and moved the people back to God's original order. Yet today, we hear so many messages along these lines that it causes one to question whether we really *do* know the voice of God.

The church of Laodicea apparently did not know the voice of God. The picture we are left with is that Jesus is knocking on the door of the Laodicean church, seeking for someone to hear His voice so He can enter. The common interpretation of this verse is that Christ is knocking on a person's heart for salvation. But in this context, Christ is not knocking on an individual's heart, but rather He is knocking on the door of the church! The church in Philadelphia submitted to His lordship, so in return, Christ is inside opening up doors:

> To the angel of the church in Philadelphia write: These are the words of him who is holy and true, who holds the key of David. What he opens no one can shut, and what he shuts no one can open. I know your deeds. See, I have placed

THE UTOPIA OF A STRANGE LOVE

before you an open door that no one can shut. I know that you have little strength, yet you have kept my word and have not denied my name. (Rev. 3:7-8)

Laodicea is totally opposite of Philadelphia. They resisted Christ's ownership, and therefore, He is outside knocking on the closed door. One might ask, If Christ is the head of the church, why does He have to knock? Christ is and will never cease being the head of the church at large. But if this particular church doesn't see their sin and need for Him, He is not going to force the door down. Eventually He will stop knocking and withdraw.

I slept but my heart was awake. Listen! My beloved is knocking: "Open to me, my sister, my darling, my dove, my flawless one. My head is drenched with dew, my hair with the dampness of the night." I have taken off my robe—must I put it on again? I have washed my feet—must I soil them again? My beloved thrust his hand through the latch-opening; my heart began to pound for him. I arose to open for my beloved, and my hands dripped with myrrh, my fingers with flowing myrrh, on the handles of the bolt. I opened for my beloved, but my beloved had left; he was gone. My heart sank at his departure. I looked for him but did not find him. I called him but he did not answer. (Song of Sol. 5:2-6)

The Christians in Laodicea are so consumed by their friendship with the world that they are not even aware Jesus is no longer "inside" the church. Without true faith, without biblical righteousness, and without spiritual insight, still they trusted in their own ability to decide matters. In Laodicea, the will of God was ultimately defined by the will and the standards of the people.

Does this sound familiar? How many churches today determine God's will in the same way? This is the fruit of a "relevant" church, self-deceived of its true condition. They believe Christ is with them because of their financial status and prestige. Their view of prosperity is distorted because God's Word and ways are not valued. If Christ is not inside their church, and if He is not Lord over their church, who gave them their wealth? Certainly not God. Will God give someone riches and fulfill their personal

A LACK OF DISCERNMENT

desires when He knows spiritually they are deceived? No, not unless He intends to judge them.

> But they soon forgot what he had done and did not wait for his plan to unfold. In the desert they gave in to their craving; in the wilderness they put God to the test. So he gave them what they asked for, but sent a wasting disease among them. (Ps. 106:13-15)

The source of their wealth is Satan, the same who, while in the wilderness with Jesus, offered Him power, dominion, and riches:

> Then Jesus was led by the Spirit into the wilderness to be tempted by the devil. After fasting forty days and forty nights, he was hungry. The tempter came to him and said, "If you are the Son of God, tell these stones to become bread." Jesus answered, "It is written: 'Man shall not live on bread alone, but on every word that comes from the mouth of God.'" Then the devil took him to the holy city and had him stand on the highest point of the temple. "If you are the Son of God," he said, "throw yourself down. For it is written: 'He will command his angels concerning you, and they will lift you up in their hands, so that you will not strike your foot against a stone.'" Jesus answered him, "It is also written: 'Do not put the Lord your God to the test.'" Again, the devil took him to a very high mountain and showed him all the kingdoms of the world and their splendor. "All this I will give you," he said, "if you will bow down and worship me." Jesus said to him, "Away from me, Satan! For it is written: 'Worship the Lord your God, and serve him only.'" (Matt. 4:1-10)

Satan tempted Jesus with turning the stone into bread, because he knew Jesus had the power to do it. Temptations are real traps to convince us to move away from the intended will of God. If Satan did not really have the power to give riches and fame, where is the test? There is a difference between the blessing of God and the reward of Satan. The enemy's rewards are designed to move a person away from God's original will. Though he is

THE UTOPIA OF A STRANGE LOVE

called "the prince of this world" (John 12:31) and "the god of this age" (2 Cor. 4:4), Satan has only limited authority. His limited authority means he can reward only with temporal things.

A Relevant Church?

Is God calling the church to bow down to the demands and needs of our surrounding culture? Is He raising up leaders who can merge the culture and Christ together? Is being "relevant" the Lord's new vision for His church? Should we have a market-driven approach to the church from the god of this age instead of a message from the Ancient of Days? To these questions the answer is clearly *no*, for if God's plan was that the church be relevant to the culture, the Son of God would have never been hung on a cross. Jesus knew very well His earthly mission was to die:

> From that time on Jesus began to explain to his disciples that he must go to Jerusalem and suffer many things at the hands of the elders, the chief priests and the teachers of the law, and that he must be killed and on the third day be raised to life. Peter took him aside and began to rebuke him. "Never, Lord!" he said. "This shall never happen to you!" Jesus turned and said to Peter, "Get behind me, Satan! You are a stumbling block to me; you do not have in mind the concerns of God, but merely human concerns." (Matt. 16:21-23)

When Moses asked Aaron why he brought great sin upon the people by fashioning a golden calf idol, Aaron turned around and blamed the people:

> [Moses] said to Aaron, "What did these people do to you, that you led them into such great sin?" "Do not be angry, my lord," Aaron answered. "You know how prone these people are to evil. They said to me, 'Make us gods who will go before us. As for this fellow Moses who brought us up out of Egypt, we don't know what has happened to him.' So I told them, 'Whoever has any gold jewelry, take it off.' Then they gave me the gold, and I threw it into the fire, and out came this calf!" (Exod. 32:21-24)

THE UTOPIA OF A STRANGE LOVE

The Israelites were determined to pursue their desires, and in his timidity, Aaron sought to please them to avoid a negative situation. The end result of all "marketing" is to satisfy both the consumer and the seller. And when this market-driven philosophy of tolerance and relevance takes over the church, God's way is forsaken in order that the people and the leadership can both be appeased. This is what happened in our Exodus story.

"Moses saw that the people were running wild and that Aaron had let them get out of control and so become a laughingstock to their enemies" (Exod. 32:25). Another verse of scripture explains this wild, uncontrollable behavior: "Where there is no revelation, people cast off restraint; but blessed is the one who heeds wisdom's instruction" (Prov. 29:18). When there is no acceptance and understanding of God's Word, even the people of God will cast off appropriate behavior and do whatever they want. It will be as in those days when Israel had no king, when "everyone did as they saw fit" (Judg. 21:25).

When church leadership abandons and undermines the Word of God, it promotes self-centered living in the people and an environment where idolatry is practiced freely and openly without any objections. Without a high and serious view of scripture, a picture of God is created that is carnal, not biblical, built of human wisdom, not Spirit inspired. When the Bible is abandoned by church leadership, people think they can be called Christians when they believe almost anything and behave in almost any way. They develop antibiblical mindsets while they are still convinced they are worshiping the God of the Bible. When people sin with no conviction of the heart, they think they can live by worldly standards and still be saved. It is a sad state of affairs when self-deception ruins souls to the extent that they find out after death that Christ never knew them:

> Not everyone who says to me, "Lord, Lord," will enter the kingdom of heaven, but only the one who does the will of my Father who is in heaven. Many will say to me on that day, "Lord, Lord, did we not prophesy in your name and in your name drive out demons and in your name perform many miracles?" Then I will tell them plainly, "I never knew you. Away from me, you evildoers!" (Matt. 7:21-23)

A LACK OF DISCERNMENT

The end result of Aaron catering to the needs of the people was that three thousand lives were lost in one day. Because of the idol, God plagued the people and withdrew His presence:

> The Levites did as Moses commanded, and that day about three thousand of the people died. Then Moses said, "You have been set apart to the Lord today, for you were against your own sons and brothers, and he has blessed you this day." The next day Moses said to the people, "You have committed a great sin. But now I will go up to the Lord; perhaps I can make atonement for your sin." So Moses went back to the Lord and said, "Oh, what a great sin these people have committed! They have made themselves gods of gold. But now, please forgive their sin—but if not, then blot me out of the book you have written." The Lord replied to Moses, "Whoever has sinned against me I will blot out of my book. Now go, lead the people to the place I spoke of, and my angel will go before you. However, when the time comes for me to punish, I will punish them for their sin." And the Lord struck the people with a plague because of what they did with the calf Aaron had made. (Exod. 32:28-35)

The story of Aaron making the idol in the wilderness shows that tolerance, self-deception, lack of discernment, and relevancy to the culture is *not* love. A passion for relevance, over and above a passion for God's Truth, is driven by *now*, rather than the ramifications of the future. It represents the spirit of Esau, who cared nothing about the eternal blessing but only what could please him at the moment:

> Once when Jacob was cooking some stew, Esau came in from the open country, famished. He said to Jacob, "Quick, let me have some of that red stew! I'm famished!" (That is why he was also called Edom.) Jacob replied, "First sell me your birthright." "Look, I am about to die," Esau said. "What good is the birthright to me?" But Jacob said, "Swear to me first." So he swore an oath to him, selling his birthright to Jacob. Then Jacob gave Esau some bread and some lentil

THE UTOPIA OF A STRANGE LOVE

stew. He ate and drank, and then got up and left. So Esau despised his birthright. (Gen. 25:29-34)

The book of Hebrews calls Esau a godless person:

See that no one is sexually immoral, or is godless like Esau, who for a single meal sold his inheritance rights as the oldest son. Afterward, as you know, when he wanted to inherit this blessing, he was rejected. Even though he sought the blessing with tears, he could not change what he had done. (Heb. 12:16-17)

Becoming ungodly, or worldly, is what happens to the church when she desires to become relevant. When worldliness enters, sound doctrine is abandoned, while the love of self is promoted. Once again, this is Laodiceanism. The desire of the Christians in Laodicea to be relevant made them useless to Christ and His kingdom. Their lukewarmness made them ineffective and undesirable, even though earthly riches were in their possession. Intellectually, they knew enough that was true to be believable, but they believed enough error to damn their souls eternally. The Laodiceans worked so hard to be relevant to their generation that they became irrelevant to the kingdom of God. In fact, their views, actions, and services made Jesus want to vomit (see Rev. 3:16 NKJV). Can it be said of the modern church that our services, activities, and beliefs are not only distasteful but disgusting to Christ? Are they an indicator that our beliefs and actions are so repulsive that we are in danger of divine rejection?

We must not be deceived by our eyes! Let us learn from history and not by experience. Paul wrote, "For everything that was written in the past was written to teach us, so that through the endurance taught in the Scriptures and the encouragement they provide we might have hope" (Rom. 15:4). He also said, "These things happened to them as examples and were written down as warnings for us, on whom the culmination of the ages has come. So, if you think you are standing firm, be careful that you don't fall!" (1 Cor. 10:11-12). Being a "relevant church" may bring us success, wealth, power, or popularity. On the other hand, there is nothing more terrifying than hearing the Lord say to us, "Depart from me."

THE MERCY OF GOD

There is a story in 2 Kings that I think parallels what is happening now in the church. It speaks about Manasseh, who reigned longer than any other king (fifty-five years), yet he was one of the most evil kings that ever lived. He rebuilt the pagan altars his father, Hezekiah, had torn down.

> He did evil in the eyes of the Lord, following the detestable practices of the nations the Lord had driven out before the Israelites. He rebuilt the high places his father Hezekiah had destroyed; he also erected altars to Baal and made an Asherah pole, as Ahab king of Israel had done. He bowed down to all the starry hosts and worshiped them. (2 Kings 21:2-3)

Manasseh's Evil Movement

King Manasseh revived the practice of soothsaying and witchcraft. We are told, "He sacrificed his own son in the fire, practiced divination, sought omens, and consulted mediums and spiritists. He did much evil in the eyes of the Lord, arousing his anger" (2 Kings 21:6). Manasseh restored Molech, the idol worship of child sacrifice, back to its popularity. He even sacrificed his own son in the fire. It is no wonder Manasseh provoked God to anger. Manasseh seduced his own people to do great evil. "Manasseh led them astray, so that they did more evil than the nations the Lord had destroyed before the Israelites" (2 Kings 21:9). Hezekiah's reformation work was eliminated in one generation by one man. Satan seduced one man to promote deceitful teachings and practices in order to deceive an entire generation.

Tradition records that during Manasseh's evil movement, he shed the blood of many who were devoted to God, and he even had the prophet Isaiah sawn in half. When those who know God are removed from the scene, such as Isaiah was, gross sin and selfish ambitions will reign. It is recorded that after Manasseh died, his son Amon ruled for two years, continuing the pattern of his father:

THE UTOPIA OF A STRANGE LOVE

> Amon was twenty-two years old when he became king, and he reigned in Jerusalem two years. His mother's name was Meshullemeth daughter of Haruz; she was from Jotbah. He did evil in the eyes of the Lord, as his father Manasseh had done. He followed completely the ways of his father, worshiping the idols his father had worshiped, and bowing down to them. He forsook the Lord, the God of his ancestors, and did not walk in obedience to him. (2 Kings 21:19-22)

John Wesley said, "What one generation tolerates, the next generation will embrace."[87] That is exactly what happened in the case of Amon. He forsook the Lord until "Amon's officials conspired against him and assassinated the king in his palace" (2 Kings 21:23). "Then the people of the land killed all who had plotted against King Amon, and they made Josiah his son king in his place" (2 Kings 21:24).

King Josiah

This was God's time now. Three hundred years earlier, it was prophesied that Josiah would rise up and bring reform:

> By the word of the Lord a man of God came from Judah to Bethel, as Jeroboam was standing by the altar to make an offering. By the word of the Lord he cried out against the altar: "Altar, altar! This is what the Lord says: 'A son named Josiah will be born to the house of David. On you he will sacrifice the priests of the high places who make offerings here, and human bones will be burned on you.'" That same day the man of God gave a sign: "This is the sign the Lord has declared: The altar will be split apart and the ashes on it will be poured out." (1 Kings 13:1-3)

Josiah led a God-ordained movement that would tear down the pagan altars, purge the land and the temple from idolatry, rebuild the altars of the Lord, remove illegitimate leadership, and restore true worship. The

---

87. Source unknown.

scriptures record that Josiah was eight years old when he became king, and he did what was right in the sight of God:

> Josiah was eight years old when he became king, and he reigned in Jerusalem thirty-one years. His mother's name was Jedidah daughter of Adaiah; she was from Bozkath. He did what was right in the eyes of the Lord and followed completely the ways of his father David,[88] not turning aside to the right or to the left. (2 Kings 22:1-2)

Josiah was the last good king before Judah went into Babylonian exile. The name Josiah is prophetic, for it means "the Lord will support" or "the Lord will heal." His birth meant God remembered His Word and would come to show He is in control. At the age of sixteen, Josiah sought the Lord wholeheartedly, and by the age of twenty, his devotion to God moved him into a radical cleansing of the land, ridding the nation from pagan worship and practices:

> In the eighth year of his reign, while he was still young, he began to seek the God of his father David. In his twelfth year he began to purge Judah and Jerusalem of high places, Asherah poles and idols. Under his direction the altars of the Baals were torn down; he cut to pieces the incense altars that were above them, and smashed the Asherah poles and the idols. These he broke to pieces and scattered over the graves of those who had sacrificed to them. He burned the bones of the priests on their altars, and so he purged Judah and Jerusalem. In the towns of Manasseh, Ephraim and Simeon, as far as Naphtali, and in the ruins around them, he tore down the altars and the Asherah poles and crushed the idols to powder and cut to pieces all the incense altars throughout Israel. Then he went back to Jerusalem. (2 Chron. 34:3-7)

---

88. Josiah was from the lineage of David and a direct descendant of Amon.

THE UTOPIA OF A STRANGE LOVE

The Book of the Law Is Found

Something that would forever change his life happened to Josiah at the age of twenty-six. While extensive repairs were being done on the house of God, after decades of neglect, a book is found:

> In the eighteenth year of his reign, King Josiah sent the secretary, Shaphan son of Azaliah, the son of Meshullam, to the temple of the Lord. He said: "Go up to Hilkiah the high priest and have him get ready the money that has been brought into the temple of the Lord, which the doorkeepers have collected from the people. Have them entrust it to the men appointed to supervise the work on the temple. And have these men pay the workers who repair the temple of the Lord—the carpenters, the builders and the masons. Also have them purchase timber and dressed stone to repair the temple. But they need not account for the money entrusted to them, because they are honest in their dealings." Hilkiah the high priest said to Shaphan the secretary, "I have found the Book of the Law in the temple of the Lord." He gave it to Shaphan, who read it. Then Shaphan the secretary went to the king and reported to him: "Your officials have paid out the money that was in the temple of the Lord and have entrusted it to the workers and supervisors at the temple." Then Shaphan the secretary informed the king, "Hilkiah the priest has given me a book." And Shaphan read from it in the presence of the king. When the king heard the words of the Book of the Law, he tore his robes. He gave these orders to Hilkiah the priest, Ahikam son of Shaphan, Akbor son of Micaiah, Shaphan the secretary and Asaiah the king's attendant: "Go and inquire of the Lord for me and for the people and for all Judah about what is written in this book that has been found. Great is the Lord's anger that burns against us because those who have gone before us have not obeyed the words of this book; they have not acted in accordance with all that is written there concerning us." (2 Kings 22:3-13)

THE MERCY OF GOD

Even in the midst of darkness and uncontrolled apostasy, God preserved a remnant of people who loved and cherished His Word enough to hide what was left of it. For almost a century, the Word of God was disregarded and abandoned, but now it is found again. After the high priest, Hilkiah, finds the Book of the Law and gives it to Josiah's scribe, Shaphan, Josiah hears the words of the book and rips his clothes as a sign of repentance and grief. King Josiah recognizes that the wrath of God was upon them because his father and grandfather violated the Word of God.

The foundation of all true reformations is seeking that which originally existed but which is now lost, discarded, or neglected. Reformation is rediscovering the original image and purpose of something—in this case, the discovery and recovery of God's Word. I believe the church is desperately in need of another reformation, not of spiritual gifts but a returning back to God-breathed scriptures. Gifts of the Spirit are very important, but the Holy Spirit will never move contrary to the Word of God. In many of our churches today, our gifts are not always accurate, and the Word we teach is distorted. But the Spirit of God is bringing order to the house of God.

How can the Great Commission—"Go and make disciples of all nations, baptizing them in the name of the Father and of the Son and of the Holy Spirit, and teaching them to obey everything I have commanded you" (Matt. 28:19-20)—be fulfilled if the houses of God are out of order? What a sad state of affairs when nonbelievers are offered salvation from sin only to be placed in unbiblical churches! In his book *Damned Through the Church*, John Warwick Montgomery said, "The church can be a place of accelerated salvation; but it can also be a place of accelerated damnation."[89] Biblical discipleship is not a formula or a training method. It does not end with the unbeliever being converted; that is only the beginning. Discipleship is a lifelong endeavor at the heart of which is sound teaching from the Bible.

The Pharisees had a form of evangelism, but Jesus did not think highly of it, to say the least. He exclaimed, "Woe to you, teachers of the law and Pharisees, you hypocrites! You travel over land and sea to win a single convert, and when you have succeeded, you make them twice as much a child of hell as you are" (Matt. 23:15). The harvest is indeed plentiful, but God is not impatient. He has a plan to grow disciples into maturity His

---

89. John Warwick Montgomery, *Damned Through The Church* (Minneapolis: Dimension Books, 1970), 24.

predetermined way—and not simply in a rush of frivolous activities to harvest those who made "decisions." The right way to do things can be reviewed in Acts 2:37-47:

> When the people heard this, they were cut to the heart and said to Peter and the other apostles, "Brothers, what shall we do?" Peter replied, "Repent and be baptized, every one of you, in the name of Jesus Christ for the forgiveness of your sins. And you will receive the gift of the Holy Spirit. The promise is for you and your children and for all who are far off—for all whom the Lord our God will call." With many other words he warned them; and he pleaded with them, "Save yourselves from this corrupt generation." Those who accepted his message were baptized, and about three thousand were added to their number that day. They devoted themselves to the apostles' teaching and to fellowship, to the breaking of bread and to prayer. Everyone was filled with awe at the many wonders and signs performed by the apostles. All the believers were together and had everything in common. They sold property and possessions to give to anyone who had need. Every day they continued to meet together in the temple courts. They broke bread in their homes and ate together with glad and sincere hearts, praising God and enjoying the favor of all the people. And the Lord added to their number daily those who were being saved.

When order is being established in the house of God, God chooses and anoints individuals to renovate old wells to rediscover forgotten truths. Before moving forward, the Spirit of God moves the church back to first principles. As history repeats itself, God will show mercy once again by bringing His people back to Him before the return of Christ. The sign of God's mercy was always the voice of the prophets.

The Prophets

Whenever God's people departed from the original divine intention, prophets were sent out to win them back from apostasy. Prophets were not sent to unbelievers but to those who had a broken covenant relationship with God. From the prophetic voice of Noah in Genesis to the prophetic warnings of Jesus in Revelation, God has always desired to turn the hearts of His people. "The Lord, the God of their ancestors, sent word to them through his messengers again and again, because he had pity on his people and on his dwelling place" (2 Chron. 36:15). It was the prophet who lent his mouth on behalf of God who stood between the mercy of God and His judgment.

Prophets were the voices God trusted in times of spiritual emergency. For every King Saul, there was a Samuel (1 Samuel 15:1-35); for every King Jeroboam, there was the young prophet and Ahijah (1 Kings 13:1-13; 14:1-18); for every King Ahab, there was an Elijah (1 Kings 18:1-45); for every King Jehoiakim, there was a Jeremiah (Jeremiah 26:1-24); and for the nation of Israel, there was a John the Baptist (Luke 3:1-20). Prophets were the alarm clocks of God, sent to awaken a people entranced in deception and worldliness. There were two responses the people could make to the prophets: wake up, or reject their message. They showed up at inconvenient times from a human point of view, but from a heavenly standpoint, they were always right on time. Prophets came to wake the people from spiritual slumber and indifference. In many cases, the prophet of God made people angry! One example of this is Herod's reaction to John the Baptist:

> Now Herod had arrested John and bound him and put him in prison because of Herodias, his brother Philip's wife, for John had been saying to him: "It is not lawful for you to have her." Herod wanted to kill John, but he was afraid of the people, because they considered John a prophet. On Herod's birthday the daughter of Herodias danced for the guests and pleased Herod so much that he promised with an oath to give her whatever she asked. Prompted by her mother, she said, "Give me here on a platter the head of John the Baptist." The king was distressed, but because of his oaths and his dinner guests, he ordered that her request be granted and had John beheaded in the prison. His head was brought in on a platter and given to the girl, who carried it to her mother. John's disciples came and took his body and buried it. Then they went and told Jesus. (Matt. 14:3-12)

THE UTOPIA OF A STRANGE LOVE

There is a common thread found among the prophets sent by God: It seems that everyone used by God in this way was out of sync with their current generation. They were not desiring to be trendy, their passion was to be trustworthy. Since the message they delivered was to God's people, what they had to say was not relevant to the wider culture. Thus they were considered unloving and critical. Vance Havner said, "God's man needs to adjust only to God's Word and God's will. It is not the business of the prophet to harmonize with the times."[90] Their message went against the current flow because it was fashioned out of a counter-cultural perspective of eternity. Ministries not running counter-culture to the current times are in danger of being self-ordained and illegitimate. In the words of author Malcolm Muggeridge, "Never forget that only dead fish swim with the stream."[91] None of God's work in the scriptures flowed from the current streams of that day. A. W. Tozer said, "I'd rather stand with God and have the world my enemy, than to go along with the crowd to destruction."[92]

When true prophetic voices are silenced or rejected, people tend to turn to those who are self-appointed. When we can freely accept and embrace a "thus said the Lord" from men God has not sent, it is a clear indication the church has dangerously backslidden. "I did not send these prophets," declares the Lord, "yet they have run with their message; I did not speak to them, yet they have prophesied. But if they had stood in my council, they would have proclaimed my words to my people and would have turned them from their evil ways and from their evil deeds" (Jer. 23:21-22).

When Hilkiah the high priest found the Book of the Law in the house of God, King Josiah instructs the priest, and a host of others, to go inquire of the Lord concerning the book, for he knew the nation had disobeyed greatly:

> He gave these orders to Hilkiah the priest, Ahikam son of Shaphan, Akbor son of Micaiah, Shaphan the secretary and Asaiah the king's attendant: "Go and inquire of the Lord for me and for the people and for all Judah about what is written

---

90. Vance Havner, *The Best of Vance Havner* (Grand Rapids: Baker Publishing Group, 1989).

91. Gregory Wolfe, *Malcolm Muggeridge Biography* (Wilmington, DE: Intercollegiate Studies Institute, 2003).

92. A. W. Tozer, *Preparing for Jesus' Return: Daily Live the Blessed Hope* (Raleigh, NC: Regal House Publishing, 2012).

> in this book that has been found. Great is the Lord's anger that burns against us because those who have gone before us have not obeyed the words of this book; they have not acted in accordance with all that is written there concerning us." (2 Kings 22:12-13)

They took the book to Huldah, the prophetess, who prophesied of the coming judgment against the nation that could not be reversed:

> Hilkiah the priest, Ahikam, Akbor, Shaphan and Asaiah went to speak to the prophet Huldah, who was the wife of Shallum son of Tikvah, the son of Harhas, keeper of the wardrobe. She lived in Jerusalem, in the New Quarter. She said to them, "This is what the Lord, the God of Israel, says: Tell the man who sent you to me, 'This is what the Lord says: I am going to bring disaster on this place and its people, according to everything written in the book the king of Judah has read. Because they have forsaken me and burned incense to other gods and aroused my anger by all the idols their hands have made, my anger will burn against this place and will not be quenched.' Tell the king of Judah, who sent you to inquire of the Lord, 'This is what the Lord, the God of Israel, says concerning the words you heard: Because your heart was responsive and you humbled yourself before the Lord when you heard what I have spoken against this place and its people—that they would become a curse and be laid waste—and because you tore your robes and wept in my presence, I also have heard you, declares the Lord. Therefore I will gather you to your ancestors, and you will be buried in peace. Your eyes will not see all the disaster I am going to bring on this place.'" So they took her answer back to the king. (2 Kings 22:14-20)

Light to Those Living in Darkness

King Manasseh's sin was so great it had reached a point of no return. Yet, because King Josiah humbled himself and was broken by the Word of God, he would be spared. Beyond this, he would witness a short time of reformation. Perhaps before the return of the Jesus, the Lord will show mercy and bring another reformation for those who have humbled themselves before God and honored His Word. But that reformation likewise will not be long term. It will not stop the end-time apostasy already in motion, but it will show humankind that God still rules from heaven, still sovereign over the universe and still in control on earth. It will also show that because the heart of God is tender and full of mercy, heaven's dawn will break open and give light to those who live in darkness under the shadow of death. It will "guide our feet into the path of peace," according to the Gospel of Luke:

> And you, my child, will be called a prophet of the Most High; for you will go on before the Lord to prepare the way for him, to give his people the knowledge of salvation through the forgiveness of their sins, because of the tender mercy of our God, by which the rising sun will come to us from heaven to shine on those living in darkness and in the shadow of death, to guide our feet into the path of peace. (Luke 1:76-79)

John the Baptist performed no miracles and spoke not one word of foretelling or prediction, and yet Jesus called John the greatest prophet born of women:

> As John's disciples were leaving, Jesus began to speak to the crowd about John: "What did you go out into the wilderness to see? A reed swayed by the wind? If not, what did you go out to see? A man dressed in fine clothes? No, those who wear fine clothes are in kings' palaces. Then what did you go out to see? A prophet? Yes, I tell you, and more than a prophet. This is the one about whom it is written: "I will send my messenger ahead of you, who will prepare your way before you." Truly I tell you, among those born of women there has not risen anyone greater than John the Baptist. (Matt. 11:7-11)

John's power as a prophet and preacher did not make him great; his greatness came from his assignment to prepare and turn the hearts of humankind to

THE MERCY OF GOD

God before the coming of Christ. The call for evangelism is just as urgent today, not only for the world but also for the house of God. The greatest harvest fields have become our pulpits and pews, and when those in the pulpits refuse to engage in sound teaching and refute false teaching, the lives of those hearing them will be repossessed. Matthew records that "Every plant that my heavenly Father has not planted will be pulled up by the roots" (Matt. 15:13).

Satan works overtime to make sure his false messengers are desensitizing the hearts of those in the church to reject the message of the true prophets and therefore to miss Christ. One cannot enjoy fellowship with the biblical Jesus but despise and shun His messengers. After Jesus appointed the seventy-two disciples to go ahead of Him to the towns He was about to go to, He told them, "Whoever listens to you listens to me; whoever rejects you rejects me; but whoever rejects me rejects him who sent me" (Luke 10:16). If we do witness a short-term reformation before the return of Jesus, the cry of repentance will be revived again, and many lives will be spared. In times of reformation, people desire to be taught:

> All the people came together as one in the square before the Water Gate. They told Ezra the teacher of the Law to bring out the Book of the Law of Moses, which the Lord had commanded for Israel. So on the first day of the seventh month Ezra the priest brought the Law before the assembly, which was made up of men and women and all who were able to understand. He read it aloud from daybreak till noon as he faced the square before the Water Gate in the presence of the men, women and others who could understand. And all the people listened attentively to the Book of the Law. Ezra the teacher of the Law stood on a high wooden platform built for the occasion. Beside him on his right stood Mattithiah, Shema, Anaiah, Uriah, Hilkiah and Maaseiah; and on his left were Pedaiah, Mishael, Malkijah, Hashum, Hashbaddanah, Zechariah and Meshullam. Ezra opened the book. All the people could see him because he was standing above them; and as he opened it, the people all stood up. Ezra praised the Lord, the great God; and all the people lifted their hands and responded, "Amen! Amen!" Then they bowed down and worshiped the Lord with their

THE UTOPIA OF A STRANGE LOVE

> faces to the ground. The Levites—Jeshua, Bani, Sherebiah, Jamin, Akkub, Shabbethai, Hodiah, Maaseiah, Kelita, Azariah, Jozabad, Hanan and Pelaiah—instructed the people in the Law while the people were standing there. They read from the Book of the Law of God, making it clear and giving the meaning so that the people understood what was being read. (Neh. 8:1- 8)

We have sacrificed and altered biblical truths at the altar of relevancy, but truths that have been discarded, overlooked, and suppressed in God's house will resurface. The Holy Spirit will resurrect "hard truth" subjects like the fear of God, the wrath of God, the lordship of Christ, repentance, biblical discipleship, and the reality of hell. Some might argue that we do not need to hear this kind of hard truth when it is God's goodness that leads one to repentance. Romans 2 has been one of the most abused scriptures in our day. Paul writes,

> Now we know that God's judgment against those who do such things is based on truth. So when you, a mere human being, pass judgment on them and yet do the same things, do you think you will escape God's judgment? Or do you show contempt for the riches of his kindness, forbearance and patience, not realizing that God's kindness is intended to lead you to repentance? But because of your stubbornness and your unrepentant heart, you are storing up wrath against yourself for the day of God's wrath, when his righteous judgment will be revealed. (Rom. 2:2-5)

The kindness of God here is not speaking about material things or the fulfillment of personal desires. This is what happens when one verse is pulled out of context to prove a point, and then the verse is divorced from the rest of the surrounding verses. Reading the Romans 2:2-5 text in its entirety, one can see why most people quote verse four and leave out the rest: "Or do you show contempt for the riches of his kindness, forbearance and patience, not realizing that God's kindness is intended to lead you to repentance?" This verse shows how God has demonstrated His kindness, leniency, and patience by withholding His judgment and the wrath we deserve. God's forbearance is extended to all before His ultimate judgment. This is what we must understand about God's goodness—it leads to repentance. There is nothing more amazing than God's goodness—but nothing more terrifying than when His goodness is abused!

Entertaining Goats and Starving Sheep

Modern-day Christians seem bored with these foundational truths. Many desire to entertain goats and starve the sheep. But my lot is with J. C. Ryle, who prophetically saw this day coming:

> There is a school of theology rising up in this day which appears to me most eminently calculated to promote infidelity, to help the devil and to ruin souls. It emphasizes that God is merciful and loving—but ignores his holiness and justice; there is much talk about heaven but none of hell; there is no mention of damnation and in the end all men and women will be saved. . . . This is a day that everybody who believes anything has faith! Everybody who thinks anything has the Spirit! Everybody is right! Nobody is wrong! . . . Reader, of all this theology I warn you solemnly to beware . . . I do believe it to be a theology that leads to hell rather than to heaven.[93]

After King Josiah heard the prophetic word, "he tore his robes" and "gave . . . orders to Hilkiah the priest, Ahikam son of Shaphan, Akbor son of Micaiah, Shaphan the secretary and Asaiah the king's attendant: 'Go and inquire of the Lord for me and for the people and for all Judah about what is written in this book that has been found.'" Then Josiah immediately gathered the people for the work of reformation:

> Then the king called together all the elders of Judah and Jerusalem. He went up to the temple of the Lord with the people of Judah, the inhabitants of Jerusalem, the priests and the prophets—all the people from the least to the greatest. He read in their hearing all the words of the Book of the

---

93. Alan Munden, "Prophetic Opinions of J. C. Ryle," article in the *Churchman*, Vol. 125/3, 2011.

THE UTOPIA OF A STRANGE LOVE

> Covenant, which had been found in the temple of the Lord. The king stood by the pillar and renewed the covenant in the presence of the Lord—to follow the Lord and keep his commands, statutes and decrees with all his heart and all his soul, thus confirming the words of the covenant written in this book. Then all the people pledged themselves to the covenant. (2 Kings 23:1-3)

Faith begins with God and not our ambition. All true faith is initiated only after God speaks. Biblical faith is not simply "stepping out," but it is responding to what the Almighty says. When Josiah and the people pledged to follow God's Covenant fully and to exalt and honor His Word, that is when the reformation began. And during reformation, when God brings things into order, He has to reveal everything that is out of order. Men with a burden from the Lord will be appointed to diagnose the ills of the house of God. Reformation in action is a movement aimed at removing corruption, faults, and defects. Josiah went back and removed the shrines and the non-Levitical priesthood established by Jeroboam three hundred years before that had caused Israel to sin:

> Just as he had done at Bethel, Josiah removed all the shrines at the high places that the kings of Israel had built in the towns of Samaria and that had aroused the Lord's anger. Josiah slaughtered all the priests of those high places on the altars and burned human bones on them. Then he went back to Jerusalem. (2 Kings 23:19-20)

The problem of unsound doctrine and the incomplete council of God we face today in the church is a centuries old one. It is a problem that great Christians of times past spoke against. Reformation is unpopular but necessary work. Canadian-American author and teacher Harry Ironside said,

> Any error, or any truth-and-error mixture, calls for definite exposure and repudiation. To condone such is to be unfaithful to God and His Word and treacherous to imperiled souls for whom Christ died. Exposing error is most unpopular work. But from every true standpoint it is worthwhile work. To our Savior, it means that He receives

from us, His blood-bought ones, the loyalty that is His due. To ourselves, if we consider 'the reproach of Christ greater riches than the treasures of Egypt,' it ensures future reward, a thousand-fold. And to souls 'caught in the snare of the fowler'—how many of them God only knows—it may mean light and life, abundant and everlasting.[94]

King Josiah's exposing and dismantling the things that caused the nation to sin earned him an honor forever recorded in the book of heaven. "Neither before nor after Josiah was there a king like him who turned to the Lord as he did—with all his heart and with all his soul and with all his strength, in accordance with all the Law of Moses" (2 Kings 23:25).

The people of God must take a heart inventory. Are we entertaining goats and starving sheep? Are we co-conspirators in carrying a distorted love message? Are we guilty of reducing the love God to something that simply meets our needs? Have we allowed ourselves to be deceived by false prophets teaching damnable doctrines? Do we financially support wolves in sheep's clothing?

The horrific thing about a heresy is that very often it is encouraging. It can draw large gatherings by uplifting the soul and calming the mind. It can promise bright futures to those who currently sit in darkness, make a heart feel peaceful, valued, and loved, and it can be seen as so admirable that people will fight for its survival. There is only one problem with a heresy: It is built on a lie and perpetuated by the devil—"When he lies, he speaks his native language, for he is a liar and the father of lies" (John 8:44).

The return of our Lord is coming soon; the church must not allow smooth sayings to harden our hearts so that we miss the moment of God's mercy. There is a contagious epidemic of strange love spreading throughout the church that will affect many for eternity. I pray my readers who see this "falling away" and who have become discouraged will rest their hearts in the word of Jude:

> To him who is able to keep you from stumbling and to present you before his glorious presence without fault and with great joy—to the only God our Savior be glory, majesty,

---

94. H. A. Ironside, "Exposing Error: Is it Worthwhile?" December 1974.

THE UTOPIA OF A STRANGE LOVE

power and authority, through Jesus Christ our Lord, before all ages, now and forevermore! Amen. (Jude 24-25)

OTHER TITLES BY WATCHMAN PUBLISHING

TAVARES D. ROBINSON

SHEPHERDS HIRELINGS AND DICTATORS

How to Recognize the Difference

10TH ANNIVERSARY EDITION

Available on Amazon.com in paperback and Kindle editions.

ISBN : 978-1732513464

Throughout generations, false prophets and insincere teachers have pretended to have the best interests of God's people in mind. They claim they are human instruments who have received direct words of the Lord through the Holy Spirit, but in the final analysis, they do not represent God.

In this tenth-anniversary edition, Pastor Robinson takes the reader on a biblical journey as he addresses many of today's toughest issues surrounding dishonest shepherds.

"Every leader should own a copy of this book. It speaks to a lot of issues taking place in the body of Christ that go undetected."

Available on Amazon.com in paperback and Kindle editions.

ISBN : 978-1732513440

Transition--a word that has become a popular buzzword in our day-- has been greatly misunderstood, some equate transition with change, but the two words do not have the same meaning. In this book Pastor Robinson details the process of the believer's transition as a necessary step for growth. Believers are often impatient and desire results immediately but God is a God of patience who takes delight that we learn from each step of thejourney.

"Understanding the process, stages, and especially the silence of God is crucial to the maturity process. This book has helped me tremendously, and I highly recommend it to those who TRULY want to grow up to the FULL stature and maturity of Christ."

Available on Amazon.com in paperback and Kindle editions.

ISBN : 978-1732513426

  The problem of deception and bowing to the culture goes all the way back to the Garden of Eden, where Adam and Eve became the Serpent's first victims. They began to see circumstances, themselves, and life in general from Satan's point of view, and God's authority was no longer the centerpiece of their lives. This book addresses the many land mines our Adversary has planted among us. It will also help readers uncover errors and recover a passion for historical biblical truths, producing a true conforming to Christ.

> *"A must-read if you yearn for a bold voice on this topic in the midst of theologically censored, commercialized, seeker-friendly fluff."*

www.ingramcontent.com/pod-product-compliance
Lightning Source LLC
Chambersburg PA
CBHW071438080526
44587CB00014B/1904